Led to Lead

Faith and Leadership Lessons from the Life of Moses

PRAISE FOR LED TO LEAD

An amazing book for small group study! *Led to Lead* brings Moses to life in twenty-two manageable lessons with answers to the challenges today's leaders face. Pastor Marty transforms the trials faced by Moses into key themes, demonstrating how Moses' personal relationship with God provided a way forward. You will feel like you know Moses at a more intimate level and will find yourself exploring how you can seek and be led by God.

Bill Adams, President and Founder
Collaborative Technical Solutions, LLC.

There is no shortage on books about leadership, but there is a dramatic shortage of leaders like Moses. So a book that recounts the exploits of this extraordinary leader; that details his unique relationship with God; that points out his flaws and explores his struggles; that explains how he learned on the job and handled wholesale resistance; that examines how he finally achieved his appointed goal but was not allowed to enjoy it, makes for compelling reading. *Led to Lead* is richly rewarding.

Stuart Briscoe, Author of Getting into God and Speaker
Telling the Truth Ministries

I've sat under Marty Berglund's ministry for over twenty years and consider him one of the finest communicators I know. Marty writes like he preaches. Always keeping his audience in mind, his passion is to make the Scriptures come alive and show their practical relevance to everyday life. *Led to Lead* is a good example of that, and well worth reading.

Dr. Dennis Borg, President and Cofounder
Integrity Ministries

I love this book! Filled with colorful stories and real-life illustrations, *Led to Lead* is a treasure trove of timeless biblical principles gleaned from an in-depth study of the life of Moses. Using his vast experience of over thirty years in pastoral ministry, Marty Berglund provides an eminently practical and unique perspective of the ways in which God worked in the life of Moses, the ways God works in our lives, and how God calls us to respond to His work in our lives. The wise biblical principles made accessible in *Led to Lead* will lead the reader into a deeper relationship with God and provide a rich understanding of God's hand in the unexpected and sometimes difficult trials of life. In addition to being a great asset for personal study and development, *Led to Lead* is an excellent resource for small group bible study

David Wiedis, J.D., M.S., Executive Director
ServingLeaders Ministries.

Led to Lead

to

Lead

Faith and Leadership Lessons from the Life of Moses

Marty Berglund

CLC PUBLICATIONS
Fort Washington, PA 19034

Led to Lead

Published by CLC Publications, U.S.A.
P.O. Box 1449, Fort Washington, PA 19034

© 2014 by CLC Publications
All rights reserved.

Printed in the United States of America

ISBN-10 (paperback): 1-61958-150-7
ISBN-13 (paperback): 978-1-61958-150-0
ISBN-13 (e-book): 978-1-61958-151-7

Originally published as Seeking the Unseen God in 2004.

TABLE OF CONTENTS

INTRODUCTION

For years I've read great books on leadership, attended great conferences and studied great leaders in both the religious and secular world. I've learned a great deal and gained great wisdom from using many sources to try and understand leadership. It's a very complex subject, and the various approaches to leadership that exist seem to be endless. Some materials I've read on leadership don't really have much to do with spiritual leadership while others can easily be transferable to church leadership and the advancement of the kingdom of God.

It seems that, in recent years, the quest for clear teaching on leadership has changed dramatically—especially within the American church. I suppose it's because of the desire to grow larger churches. The examples used in seminar after seminar and conference after conference, as well as in numerous books, are generally not from the perspective of the spiritual side of leadership, but mostly from the managerial, administrative and visionary side. If you participated in many of the church conferences held in recent years, you were likely persuaded that following God's call for your church was mostly about methodology and techniques that, if employed, would cause your church to be blessed with both growth and spiritual vibrancy.

After being a pastor for over thirty years and attending some of those conferences, I now realize I need much more than they ever gave me. In short, I need more of God. Yes, I do need leadership principles on governance and models of outreach assimilation and how to grow healthy disciples. I do need the inspiring examples of growing churches and strong leaders. But I believe I need most what is so desperately lacking in America today: spiritual leadership with the emphasis being on the spiritual.

There are leaders of churches that people consider quite successful, but who are not very spiritual men. They are not godly in their methods, teaching, attitudes or behavior. They may lead well, but they don't spiritually lead very well at all. Over the years, I've even had some of them confess to me their deep spiritual poverty. What they hunger to learn is spiritual leadership not just leadership in general. Jesus told His disciples they were "not of this world." That was, along with other inferences, in order to instruct them that their leadership style would be born from a spiritual rather than natural model.

Church leadership conferences nowadays seem to teach little on how to walk in the Spirit or how to know God's calling. There is minimal emphasis on how to pray through difficult problems or how to structure your staff so they follow God. In reading a recent book on church history over the last 200 years, I was struck by how the stuff we talk about and study and preach in our conferences today are things serious followers of God in the past would have considered unimportant. Instead, they would be seeking to be spiritual first and be leaders second. We, on the other hand, have made being a leader our primary concern and being spiritual secondary—if pursued at all.

In my hunger and concern for spiritual leaders, I've also had many friends who have suffered tragic consequences because they grew great ministries but didn't lead themselves or others to great spirituality. One friend in ministry became addicted to drugs in order to cope with his pressures. I performed his funeral as he left behind a wife and three children. Another friend wrote me a great letter of thanks even though I hadn't talked to him in years. He then proceeded to jump out of a hotel window to his death. I performed his funeral as well. I've also had numerous friends commit adultery, become addicted to pornography and even take money from the churches they led. How, I ask myself, did such great men become seduced by sin? How did guys I thought were strong spiritually become so weak? The answer is this: They became leaders—really good leaders—but they didn't become spiritual leaders.

My hope is that this little book about Moses will help you to grow in becoming a spiritual leader—no matter who you are or what you do. I am always shocked by how many of those in the church who study leadership never think to study Moses, one of the greatest leaders in all human history. He was a man who led well over a million people out of slave captivity and into a wilderness, later setting them up to become a nation of their own. All of this was done primarily because of God's work in his life. Moses was a very reluctant leader. He often lacked the skill, techniques and methodology to lead well. And yet, he did. How? The simple yet very complex answer is…God.

I truly hope this book can help you to find God in your complex world. Moses found God in his world, having more responsibilities and more pressures than any of us will ever face. Maybe by studying Moses you can learn how to find God's calling for your life, as well as learn how to follow Him as you lead others. That's my hope and prayer for you. May God bless you and guide you as you read, and may you become the spiritual leader God has called you to be as a disciple of Jesus Christ.

Pastor Marty Berglund

Chapter 1

Going Deeper

Home ownership has its challenges, and I experienced one of the biggest a few years ago. I went to take a shower one day, but when I turned on the faucet, all I got was a trickle. I thought maybe it was nothing more than a clogged shower head, but when I turned on the sink downstairs it was the same thing: The water was just trickling out. I thought, *Oh boy, I've got a problem.*

Fortunately, I just happen to live across the street from a well-drilling company. They checked it out and said, "Your water pump is full of sand; you're sucking dirt. With a well this shallow, you are never going to get the kind of pressure you want. We recommend that you go deeper."

I had a choice, didn't I? I could live on a trickle or I could go deeper. Many Christians face the same choice in their relationships with God. They can either live on the trickle that they get from a church service on Sunday, or they can decide to place their faith in God daily and live by the principles of His Word.

Take, for example, the following biblical promise: God works on behalf of the faithful. It is a wonderful truth, a principle that is taught throughout Scripture, but it doesn't do you any good if you don't believe it. A lot of people—even church-going people—don't really believe it, or at best, they are struggling to believe it.

This brings to mind the words of a friend who revealed to me that his wife had cheated on him. He said, "Marty, I was faithful, and she still had an affair. It doesn't look like God worked on my behalf." Another friend of mine told me, "I was faithful to my company. I was a loyal employee. I gave them my time, my energy; I gave them everything. They still stole my patents; they still demoted me; they still cut my salary. It doesn't look like God worked on my behalf."

Then there's the story we heard a while ago about the missionary plane that was shot down by the Peruvian Air Force, which mistook them for drug smugglers. A woman missionary and her infant were killed.

I know that many people could tell stories of how their faithfulness was rewarded by God; I could too. We could tell story after story, but does it always look like God works on behalf of the faithful? It doesn't, does it? A woman in our church developed a brain tumor a few years ago—a cancer of the most aggressive type—and we thought we were going to lose her. What do you do when you are faced with something like that in your own life? Will you continue to live on a trickle, or will you go deeper?

This woman with the tumor hit that wall of decision; she had to make that choice. When it didn't seem like God was working on her behalf, she said to herself, "I have a choice; I can live the rest of my life on a trickle or I can go deeper." She chose to go deeper. And today she is a victor over cancer.

I know Christians who live for years and years on a trickle because they hit some crisis and became confused. "Why, God? Why don't you take care of this? It doesn't look like You are working on behalf of me, and I'm being faithful." And they decide to just live like that, in despair and confusion—maybe even depression.

You have a choice before you. If you want to live on a trickle, I really can't help you. But if you want to go deeper, take a look with me at the story of Moses, which begins in Exodus 1.

A MAN WORTHY OF STUDY

I wonder how many people recognize what a significant person Moses is in human history. A prophet and teacher of immeasurable influence, his instructions from thousands of years ago formed the basis of the Judeo-Christian ethic, as well as the legal systems of the United States and many other countries—and yet, of course, the instructions were the Lord's message through him.

Many also consider Moses to be one of the greatest leaders of all human history. After all, he took a couple of million people out of captivity in Egypt and into freedom almost single-handedly—and yet, of course, it was the Lord working through him.

That is the secret that makes this man worthy of study. The teachings and the life of Moses are powerful because he was a man who claimed to know God. He even talked to the Lord face-to-face. If you want to know and understand more about God, you've got to know something about Moses. If you don't know about Moses, you are sadly ignorant.

Just like you and me, Moses was born into a situation—a set of circumstances, an historical period. In fact, many of the things surrounding him were very crucial. His parents, his siblings, his friends, his enemies, his heritage, the government under which he was born—all these things influenced him just like they influence you and determine who you are. As we look at the period in which Moses was born, we can see how God was at work to prepare mankind for the birth of this person who was going to be used so powerfully in the history of mankind. Moses was born at a time of crisis—a crisis in the government, among his people, in his family. The first chapter of Exodus shows how God was at work, even in a crisis time, among those who were faithful. If you have ever been abused, mistreated, overlooked or taken for granted, you can understand the situation into which Moses was born. You may also be able to understand how important it is in the midst of that kind of crisis to be faithful. Because of the faithfulness of a handful of people, Moses was brought into this world. What they did in their faith, God used.

Whether or not you are in a crisis right now, the principle taught in Exodus 1, that God works on behalf of the faithful, is a message for you—that is, if you dare to believe it.

EVEN WHEN THINGS SEEM THEIR WORST

God works on behalf of the faithful even when things seem their worst. And that's what happened in Exodus. You may recall from the end of Genesis that Joseph had risen to power in Egypt and invited his whole family to come there and survive the famine. Exodus continues the story of this amazing clan: "Then Joseph died, and all his brothers and all that generation" (1:6). Hundreds of years had passed and that first generation was long gone. But God continued to bless Israel: "But the people of Israel were fruitful and increased greatly; they multiplied and grew exceedingly strong, so that the land was filled with them" (1:7). It has been estimated that there were probably 2 to 3 million Israelites living in Egypt at that time. The land was filled with them.

But the next verse (1:8) signals a change in the fortunes of the children of Israel: "Now there arose a new king over Egypt, who did not know Joseph." Historians tell us this new king was probably a member of the Hyksos—an Asiatic tribe that developed the compound bow and iron chariots. With this advanced weaponry, they were able to conquer Egypt, the superpower of the day. This is how a king could come to power who "did not know Joseph." Let's look at the context:

> Now there arose a new king over Egypt, who did not know Joseph. And he said to his people, "Behold, the people of Israel are too many and too mighty for us. Come, let us deal shrewdly with them, lest they multiply, and, if war breaks out, they join our enemies and fight against us and escape from the land." (Exod.1:8–10)

When this new king from the outside comes into power, he knows nothing about Joseph; he simply notices this large group of powerful, unified people in his land and sees them as a threat. He may have heard some of the stories we read in Genesis. The Israelites were notoriously strong people. It makes him nervous. So he decides to "deal shrewdly with them." And here is his plan: "Therefore they set taskmasters over them to afflict them with heavy burdens. They built for Pharaoh store cities, Pithom and Raamses" (1:11).

In the ancient world, this was a common leadership tactic. If there was somebody under your rule who scared you, you just enslaved them and worked them like dogs. Can you imagine the situation? You are on a labor gang, climbing up some stinking pyramid all day in the middle of one hundred-degree weather, sweating all day in the dirt; you come home dog-tired. The strategy was to work them so hard that they wouldn't have time to reproduce—and it was usually successful.

Verse 12, however, significantly begins with the word but: "But the more they were oppressed, the more they multiplied and the more they spread abroad. And the Egyptians were in dread of the people of Israel." The tactic had just the opposite effect on Israel, which I believe was an act of God. History shows that other peoples, some greater and stronger than the Israelites, were defeated this way—subjugated and literally ruled out of history. We don't even know their names anymore. But when the Israelites were put in slave labor, they just kept growing. It was the way God honored the children of

Israel for their faithfulness in worshipping Him and refusing to worship the pharaoh, as all of Egypt did.

This little window into ancient history shows how God works on behalf of the faithful. It's a miracle taking place right before us. I'm sure that during that time, the Israelites were asking the same kinds of questions that some of my friends have asked: "Where is God in all this? Here I am with my leg chained to some other guy as we slave away building this pyramid. Where is God?" And yet they continued to grow and their families were blessed by God.

Years ago, my wife and I moved into a new development and became friends with another couple in the neighborhood. They were about our age and they started having kids about the same time we did. They ended up having three girls, just like we did. The husband seemed to be climbing the ladder in his business, so it wasn't long before he had a job change and they moved away. After a few more relocations, they ended up living in North Jersey and he began a new job in New York City.

As we renewed contact with them through letters and phone calls (this was before e-mail), my wife and this guy's wife, Mary Jo, became very good friends. When she had lived in our neighborhood, Mary Jo had come to our Bible studies and heard the gospel. In the midst of all the different moves, she had become a Christian.

Her spouse, however, took a different path. After they had been in New Jersey for a while, this man decided he no longer wanted to live with his wife and little girls. He left them to live with another woman in New York City.

Faced with an overwhelming crisis, Mary Jo was asking the same kinds of questions: "Where's God? I've been used to living on a healthy income; now I have to leave my house and move into a little apartment. I've got three girls under eight years old. I've got to find a job and get a baby sitter for my kids. I thought God worked on the behalf of the faithful, but things seem to be getting worse and worse."

And just as she seemed to be getting back on her feet, the baby sitter quit. Have you ever experienced that kind of situation, where something bad happens in your life and then something else happens and then something more happens? Sometimes problems seem to come in piles like that. I think true maturity is the person who can watch it all pile up and still be faithful. Mary Jo was having trouble doing that.

On the day the baby sitter quit, Mary Jo decided, "OK, I'm going to go to church." At a small-group meeting that night, she began sharing her situation: "So here I am with no baby sitter and my three girls to take care of. I don't know how I'm going to be able to keep my job. I don't understand what's going on. What do I do?"

She told us later, "By the time I walked out of the church that night"—she started crying as she was telling us—"four different people came to me and said, 'I'll baby sit your kids.' These were people I would love to leave my kids with.

"I came out of that meeting realizing that God does care, God does love me, God is going to watch out for me if I continue to be faithful. Up until that point I felt like kicking God in the face because I felt like I was being faithful, but He wasn't taking care of me. The crisis came that night, when I realized I have a choice. I can either live on a trickle or I can go deeper. I can keep kicking God in the face or I can just decide to trust Him."

We could just see when we talked with her that a change had happened in her life—a change of heart. Today, Mary Jo is remarried to a wonderful guy and lives in Colorado. Her girls are all grown up and things turned out great. But it all started at that crisis point when Mary Jo made the decision, "I'm just going to be faithful and go deeper. I'm confused, I don't understand why all this had to happen to me, but I'm deciding to be faithful."

And just as He did with the Israelites, God honors that faithfulness. Even in the midst of opposition, when it looks insurmountable, when things seem to be getting worse and piling up, God works on behalf of the faithful.

EVEN WHEN YOU'RE A "NOBODY"

At some point in this first part of Exodus, historians tell us, the Egyptians kicked out the Hyksos tribe and their own pharaohs took over again. Apparently, when they were back in power the new pharaoh said, "I like having these Israelites as slaves. In fact, let's tighten the screws a little." The situation got worse, not better!

But God continued to work on behalf of the faithful, even those who were considered "nobodies." We see this in the story of the Hebrew midwives:

> Then the king of Egypt said to the Hebrew midwives, one of whom was named Shiphrah and the other Puah, "When you serve as midwife to the Hebrew women and see them on the birthstool, if it is a son, you shall kill him, but if it is a daughter, she shall live." But the midwives feared God and did not do as the king of Egypt commanded them, but let the male children live. So the king of Egypt called the midwives and said to them, "Why have you done this, and let the male children live?"
>
> The midwives said to Pharaoh, "Because the Hebrew women are not like the Egyptian women, for they are vigorous and give birth before the midwife comes to them."
>
> So God dealt well with the midwives. And the people multiplied and grew very strong. And because the midwives feared God, he gave them families. (Exod. 1:15–21)

The new pharaoh told the midwives to kill all the male babies, but the Hebrew midwives feared God and decided not to do it. And when asked why, I don't think they really lied when they said, "These women are tougher than Egyptian women" (see Exod. 1:19). My wife says that when she lived in Vietnam, she saw it happen. The Vietnamese women working in the rice paddies would go over to the side, squat, have a baby, clean it off, strap it onto their back and go back to the rice paddy. That must have been what the Israelite women were like.

Anyway, that's the excuse they gave the pharaoh, and he bought it. And as a result of their faithfulness, "God dealt well with the midwives" (Exod. 1:20)—probably by sparing their lives, by not letting the pharaoh kill them. It goes on to say, "And because the midwives feared God, he gave them families" (1:21). God personally blessed them for their faithfulness. And yet, who were these midwives? Nobodies! God will even be faithful on behalf of nobodies.

The same scenario is found in chapter 2 when Moses was born. I believe Moses was the sign of God's faithfulness to a pair of faithful people—his parents, who were a couple of nobodies. And yet, even though the Israelites were faithful and the midwives were faithful, it still got worse: "Then Pharaoh commanded all his people, 'Every son that is born to the Hebrews you shall cast into the Nile, but you shall let every daughter live'" (1:22). Why in the world would the Egyptians put up with an order like this? For one thing, they believed Pharaoh was a god; for another, they worshipped the Nile River. And so to sacrifice their infant sons in the Nile River was not ludicrous in their minds. Such human sacrifices took place in those days.

It was in the midst of that crisis that Moses' parents, who already had an eight-year-old girl and a three-year-old boy, found out they were pregnant. You think perhaps they were praying for a girl? You bet they were. But they had a boy. What were they going to do?

They decided to be faithful. And their faithfulness caused Moses to be saved from death. I believe God honored their faithfulness and worked on their behalf and on behalf of all Israel; in fact, He worked on behalf of the whole human race, because Moses was so influential. This blessing, this work of God—Moses being born—was a result of faithfulness on the part of Moses' parents.

In the midst of studying Moses, I read a book called *Reaching for the Invisible God: What Can We Expect to Find?* by Philip Yancey, in which he discusses the issue of staying faithful even when things go from bad to worse. He says that staying faithful means accepting that we cannot answer the "why" questions. You just aren't smart enough because you are not God. Sooner or later, as a human, you've got to realize how dumb you are. You're not going to know why till you get to glory.

At the end of one chapter, Yancey tells about a Scottish preacher in the last century who lost his wife suddenly. After her death, he preached an unusually personal sermon. He admitted in the message that he did not understand this life of ours, but still less could he understand how people facing loss could abandon faith. "Abandon it for what?" he said. "You people in the sunshine may believe the faith, but we in the shadows must believe it. We have nothing else." [i]

That's what it came down to for the Israelites, and that's what it came down to for Moses' parents. That's why they wrapped their baby and put him into the water. They were just trusting God. The question we come down to is this: Are you going to continue to live on a trickle of doubt and despair and depression, or are you going to go deeper? I challenge you even in the midst of all the "why" questions. You're never going to answer them all; you don't have sufficient data to come to a conclusion. There comes a point when you have to say, "I'm going to believe God and His revealed truth and all that He has done in my life. I will be faithful."

For you, it may mean being faithful in your marriage. It may mean being faithful to the company and not bad-mouthing the boss. It may mean being faithful with your money and continuing to give in the midst of a financial trial. You're going to be faithful because you trust God—that's what faith is all about. It's how you truly connect with God.

No matter who you are, you are going to be tested in your faith. Whether it's a clogged sink, a flat tire or something more serious like contracting cancer, you'll be tested; everyone is. The question is, will you live on a trickle or will you go deeper?

What Does Faith Look Like?

The theme of God working on behalf of the faithful carries into the second chapter of Exodus, with even more detail, since faithfulness simply comes down to faith. "Full of faith" is what faithfulness means. One question remains, however: What does faith look like in someone's life?

In the lives of Moses' parents in Exodus chapter 2, we see real-life faith demonstrated in a very powerful way. And I hope that through us looking at this story you can begin to see what faith might look like in your life. A tragic thing happens to us as Christians: We come to church, we call ourselves Christians, we read the Bible, but when it comes to putting faith into practice, we miss the connection. Sometimes, though, by looking at it in someone else's life, in a real-life story, we can regain the connection.

The story of the Hebrews in the book of Exodus is a story of God directly corresponding with people. He's in an unseen world that they can't experience, but God is touching them, and they are touching God. Scripture reveals that the only way to be in connection with this unseen world is through faith. And in this story (2:1–10) you see demonstrated faith in real life—the real life of Moses' parents.

The Hebrew people had lived in Egypt for four hundred years—they were well ingrained. And the sad truth is that many of them had given up following Yahweh and were now following the god of the Nile, along with the other gods of the Egyptians. In fear of Pharaoh they submitted to his leadership, because they found that life went better in Egypt if they did. We can't begin to imagine some of the social pressures they had bowed to.

But there were two people we know of who resisted following the Egyptian way and were faithful to God: the parents of Moses. From another passage (Num. 26:59) we learn that the father was Amram and the mother was Jochebed.

I'm sure that Pharaoh's edict (to throw every male child in the Nile) came to Jochebed's and Amram's minds when they realized she was pregnant. And when the day came that she could feel the birth pains start, I'm sure she was praying, *Oh Lord, let it be a girl. Let it be a girl.* Can you imagine how she felt when she saw it was a boy? Joy and fear must have collided in her heart. One thing we do know: The text says that when she saw the baby, she saw that he was beautiful (see Exod. 2:2, NKJV). She was in love with him from the very beginning.

I wonder, did God put that in her heart? He must have caused her to so fall in love with this little baby at first sight that she thought, No! *No way can I sacrifice this baby. No one is going to take this baby from me!* Of course, most mothers would feel like that—it's their baby, their little boy. So Jochebed and Amram hid the baby for three months. (Can you imagine? I'll bet he was the fattest little baby in the world, because every time he started to cry, she probably fed him to keep him quiet!)

They were taking a great risk; it could mean death to defy the government and the pharaoh. Remember, the Egyptians were the same people who sacrificed humans in the Nile. They wouldn't have thought twice about wiping out the whole family.

For three months they hid him, trying to keep it quiet. We don't know why they gave up hiding him; maybe Amram finally put his foot down and said, "We can't go on like this;

our whole family is threatened." Maybe God spoke to them and showed them what to do; we aren't told.

But we do know what happened next: Jochebed found a basket woven out of bulrushes with a cover on it, and she coated it with pitch, top and bottom, so it would float. Then she wrapped her little baby boy in a blanket, put him in the basket and put the basket in the reeds along the Nile River. And she left him there (see Exod. 2:3). Can you imagine how she felt? As she turned around and walked home, the tears must have been streaming down her face; it must have ripped her heart out to leave her little boy.

The Bible says that when Jochebed left Moses in the reeds, "His sister stood at a distance to know what would be done to him" (Exod. 2:4). We don't know if she was supposed to be there or not. Did her mother say, "Watch and see what happens to the baby," or did she just sneak down there and hide in the reeds? We don't know. But we do know the rest of the story, because this little girl was there watching.

Pharaoh's daughter, the princess, came down to the river to bathe. She was probably bathing in the Nile as a medicinal or religious ritual, for she had private baths to bathe in. She came with an entourage of maids and servants—after all, she was a princess—and when she saw the basket lying in the reeds, she told a maidservant to bring it over to her. The princess set the basket down and took the cover off. "Oh, look at this baby. This is one of the Hebrew babies."

Perhaps it was the light shining in the baby's eyes, or maybe the rustling of the basket woke him up; anyway, the baby started to cry, so she picked him up. And that probably did it! Once you pick up a baby and hold him, you're hooked. Some have suggested that she had problems having children herself; we don't know. But all of a sudden, out of nowhere, she began having these maternal feelings. And she said, "This baby is mine— finders, keepers."

Then Moses' big sister saw her chance, so she ran over and said, "Your Highness, would you like one of the Hebrew women to nurse that baby for you?"

"Yes," answered the princess. "Go get someone immediately; the baby's hungry."

Can you imagine the scene? The girl runs home as fast as her little legs can carry her. "Mom! Mom!" she cries as she runs into the house. "You won't believe it! The princess came down to the Nile, found the basket and opened it up. She's holding the baby, Mom! She wants you to come and nurse him. I didn't tell her that you're the mother; I just offered to get someone to take care of him. Come on, Mom, let's go!" I'm sure she was speaking so fast and so excitedly that her mother didn't know what she was talking about at first.

Can you imagine what Jochebed was feeling? She had just started to deal with the pain of giving up her baby when suddenly her daughter came in with this fantastic story! As she ran down to the river, she was probably trying to calm down so that she wouldn't give herself away.

Walking up to the princess, she said, "Your Highness, I would be glad to care for that baby for you." And the princess put the baby into her arms and said, "Fine. Go nurse this baby and I'll pay you." (Wow! That's pretty good—getting paid to nurse your own baby.) "And when he's weaned, bring him back to me."

Imagine what was going on in Jochebed's heart and mind! She had just given up her baby. (I don't think she was abandoning the baby; there's just too much care put into that basket. Maybe they had some kind of plan in mind, or maybe God just told her to do this.) And now she was walking back home with her child in her arms! She must have been thinking, *O Lord, I can't believe what You've done! I've resisted following the Egyptian way and I put my trust in You, hoping that somehow You'd do something. But I never expected something like this to happen!*

So she went back home and cared for the baby—we don't know for how long, but probably a few years. She nursed him, trained him and probably taught him about the Lord. She kept him as long as she possibly could. And then the day came when she had to take her little boy, now a toddler, to the palace and say, "Here he is; I'm finished"—the second time she had to give away her little boy. Only a mother could understand that. It must have been devastating.

There are a number of lessons in faith that we can learn from what these people were doing and how they trusted God. What does faith look like in real life? You can see it in the real lives of Jochebed and Amram.

FAITH RESISTS

The first faith lesson we can learn is this: If you are really going to have faith, you will have to resist some other things, such as doubts, unbelief and the pressure to conform to the culture around you. Amram and Jochebed did a lot of resisting. Hebrews 11:23 says, "By faith Moses, when he was born, was hidden for three months by his parents, because they saw that the child was beautiful, and they were not afraid of the king's edict."

The key words in this passage are faith and not afraid. You can't have faith and still have fear. Fear is against faith; the two are not compatible within the same soul. And yet, many Christians try to live with both. But you can't do it. You have to either resist the faith or resist the fear.

Amram and Jochebed chose to resist the fear and take the faith—faith in Yahweh, the God of the Hebrew people, the true God, not the false gods of Egypt. That took some resistance. It's a powerful thing to decide not to go along with the compromising of the moral culture, with the ethical rationalization that's around us.

It's the same today as it was in Egypt—rationalization and compromise. Christians are tempted day in and day out to succumb to it—at their jobs, at school, in their families, with friendships, in the neighborhood. True faith requires some resistance; you have to stand on the truth. Amram and Jochebed were willing to do that. They could have been afraid of the king, their neighbors, other gods, their future—but they stood their ground and God honored it.

I prayed recently with someone who worries that she won't ever get married; she has a great fear of that. But what do you do, follow the fear or follow faith in God? That's the choice; you have to resist one or the other. Another person I talked to the other day was very fearful financially. Have you ever been in that position—fearful that you're not going to make it?

It is interesting how fear and money go hand in hand. When you don't have money, you're afraid you're not going to get any; when you do have money, you're afraid you're going to lose it! That may be one of the reasons money causes so many problems in our lives and becomes such a god over us: It causes us to be afraid. And when we spend all our time in fear, not in faith, it dominates us. If we want to regain our freedom, it's going to take some resistance.

I talked to someone a while ago who is afraid of getting cancer because of something the doctor said. Maybe you're afraid of some disease coming into your life or your loved one's life. Or maybe you're afraid for your children. There are a lot of things to be afraid of; the world we live in incites fear. The world back in Moses' day was no different than the world today. And what we're challenged to do as Christians is to believe that we can correspond with a God in the unseen world who can change that. Jochebed was willing to do that.

A man in my church told me that as he started his business with his son, he had this great fear that it wasn't going to work out. He was delighted as they began to get job after job and things started coming together. "Then," he continued, "the fear started, because we started losing money. And one particular contractor with whom we did a lot of business didn't pay us. The next thing we knew, we weren't able to pay our bills."

His next statement surprised me: "This is the best thing that ever happened to me! For the first time in my life, I realize what it means to truly trust God. I just had to come to a place of abandoning myself to Him. I needed this in my life."

Maybe you need such a thing in your life. I wonder if that's why God allowed Amram and Jochebed to face such a difficult situation. The same may be true of the situations we face in our lives. God is dead serious about us learning to know Him—and we're only going to do that through faith. It's going to take resistance—resisting fear, temptations, compromise, rationalization. If you can resist, you can have faith. If you can't resist, it's going to be difficult, because faith and fear don't go together in the human soul.

FAITH HOPES

The second principle we learn from Amram and Jochebed is that faith hopes. Jochebed's story is all about hope, isn't it? She hid the baby in the hope that somehow they would be able to keep him. She put the baby in a basket covered with tar and put him in the Nile by the reeds in the hope that—well, we don't know. I don't think she knew everything that was going to happen. But she did that in hope.

Faith and fear don't go together well in the human soul, but faith and hope go together beautifully. In the New Testament, the word for faith and the word for hope are almost synonymous. I don't think it's possible to have one without the other.

A former teacher of mine, psychiatrist Frank Minirth, used to say that the first step for anyone to get better is to have hope. Many people have surrendered to despair and depression and think they can't get better. The number one priority, Minirth says, is to help them realize that there is a God who cares and that they can have hope.

Donald Grey Barnhouse, while on a trip to Japan, had an experience that brought home to him the uniqueness of the Christian's hope:

> In the lobby in the Imperial Hotel in Tokyo, Japan, the girl at one of the airline desks spoke Chinese, Japanese and English. She was obviously from a cultured background. I asked her if she was a Christian. She replied that she was a Buddhist. Further questions enlisted the information that she had heard of Christ and knew that there was a sacred book called the Bible, but she had never read it, and knew nothing of the Christian truth. I then asked her a question. "Do you love Buddha?" "Love? I never thought about love in connection with religion." I said to her, "Do you know then in the whole world no god is truly loved except the Lord Jesus Christ? Other gods are hated and feared. You have statues of fierce monsters to guard the gates of your temples. And the people stand at a distance and try to awaken their gods by clapping their hands. They burn incense and offer sacrifices to them as though their gods had to be appeased. But Jesus Christ loves us."[ii]

Dr. Barnhouse went on to patiently explain that Muslims do not love Allah, and Hindus and Buddhists do not love their gods. But Christians love God because, as it says in First John 4:19, "We love because he first loved us."

We have hope because we have a God who loves us—"For God so loved the world" (John 3:16). The God of the Old Testament is the same God. Amram and Jochebed were counting on a God who would do something for their little baby, a God who would touch their lives. They had hope because they had a God who cared. You have that God too, if you trust in Jesus Christ as your Savior and Lord. He loves you, He cares for you; there is never a reason you shouldn't have hope as a Christian. "And we know that for those who love God all things work together for good, for those who are called according to his purpose" (Rom. 8:28). His purpose is to fulfill His love in your life.

FAITH ENTRUSTS

If you have faith you will also learn to entrust. The most important issue, however, is the object of your trust. We can see that in this story. Did Jochebed entrust that child to the Nile River? No. She entrusted him to God as she put him in the basket. Did she entrust that little toddler into the hands of the princess? No. She entrusted him into the hands of God as she gave him to the princess.

That distinction is very important, because you and I have the same kind of decision to make every day. Do you entrust your happiness in your marriage to your spouse? No. You entrust your happiness in your marriage to God, and maybe He'll use your spouse. Do you entrust your happiness to the government? No. You entrust your happiness to God, and maybe He'll use the government. Do you entrust your health to your doctor? No. You entrust your health to God, and maybe He'll use the doctor.

I don't know about you, but when I'm sitting in a doctor's office or a dentist's chair, I'm praying, *Lord, please help this guy do the right thing.* I guess I've been around too many people. People are people, and they make mistakes, but God doesn't. And He's my God, so I'm going to entrust myself to Him. He could use any good doctor or not even use a doctor at all. That part doesn't matter as long as I entrust myself to God.

Hebrews tells us what great faith Jochebed and Amram had. I think they were at the place where they could say, "In spite of the circumstances, in spite of anyone's mistakes or evil intentions, I can trust God." Can you do that?

If you can't, maybe it's because you need to get a bigger concept of God. We often try in vain to envision a God who we can manipulate—one very much like ourselves, who cuts us a break every time we "need" it. We want God, but we settle for our own control instead. But isn't the whole point of trusting God that we're not in control anymore?

To experience the grace of God in your life is to admit who He is and who you are. It's to admit His greatness and His mystery, that you can't comprehend it all and you won't know all the answers. But you can entrust yourself to God because what is revealed about Him tells you that He loves you and He works in an unseen way in your life—even through other people who He puts over you.

That's the message behind the story of the centurion who asked Jesus to heal his servant:

> When he had entered Capernaum, a centurion came forward to him, appealing to him, "Lord, my servant is lying paralyzed at home, suffering terribly." And he said to him, "I will come and heal him." But the centurion replied, "Lord, I am not worthy to have you come under my roof, but only say the word, and my servant will be healed. For I too am a man under authority, with soldiers under me. And I say to one, 'Go,' and he goes, and to another, 'Come,' and he comes, and to my servant, 'Do this,' and he does it." When Jesus heard this, he marveled and said to those who followed him, "Truly, I tell you, with no one in Israel have I found such faith." (Matt. 8:5–10)

Why was Jesus so impressed by the centurion's faith? Because this man believed God could work through the authority put over him. Some of the greatest faith you can demonstrate is to believe that God can work through your boss, your husband, your government. God can work through those in authority over you. The temptation is to gripe and complain, to be bitter and angry. Those are acts of unbelief. The person who really believes says, "No, I can entrust myself to God."

Jochebed and Amram did that with their boy, and he became the leader who shut down Egypt, the one who told Pharaoh, "Let my people go!" Who knows what your child could do? Who knows what you could do, if you could believe God? Jesus said if you have faith like a tiny mustard seed, you could move a whole mountain (see Matt. 17:20). It's just a matter of putting a faith that resists, hopes and entrusts into your life.

Chapter 3

What Are You Living For?

If I wanted to get to know you, we would sit down together and I would say, "Tell me about yourself. Where did you grow up? What school did you go to? Tell me about your parents, your brothers and sisters. Where do you work? Are you married? How many kids do you have?" and so on. I would ask those kinds of questions, you would share with me the answers and we would get to know each other, right?

Well, it doesn't work that way with God. If we came before God and said, "God, tell me about Yourself," He might say, "There was a man named Moses." And if we asked, "Why would You tell me about Moses when I asked about You?" He would answer, "Because you're just a mere human being. How could you know the invisible God? You can't comprehend Me in your little mind." To understand God, we have to see Him in human terms. We can get to know God from seeing Moses' life, which is why it is recorded in divine revelation for us.

Scripture doesn't reveal a lot about Moses' childhood, his teen years or even his twenties and thirties. But we can speculate a lot from what has been revealed. In Acts 7 Stephen tells us a little bit about Moses: "Moses was instructed in all the wisdom of the Egyptians" (7:22). The Egyptians had a very advanced culture, so that's saying quite a lot. The same verse adds that he "was mighty in his words and deeds," which tells us something about his leadership skills.

Growing up in the palace in Egypt, you understand, was like growing up in the White House. Egypt was the most powerful nation in the world at that time, and Moses was in the top of the top. He grew up in luxury, raised by the princess herself and considered her son—a very privileged background.

From what ethnologists have discovered, little boys at his age had shaved heads with a strand of braided hair coming down the side. We know too that as a little boy in the privileged class, Moses had lots of toys. Archeologists have discovered that some Egyptian children had elaborate spinning tops. They even have found a set of dancing men—an elaborate mechanical toy (the Egyptians were advanced engineers) that could dance on a hard surface when you pulled the string. I'm sure Moses had one. After all, as the princess' son, he could have anything he wanted.

We also know that, like other ruling-class boys his age, Moses participated in sports—swimming, horseback riding and archery. We know he had fun times going places and doing things. He probably even had a house pet or two. Aside from video games and computers, his life doesn't sound that much different from an American kid's, does it? Of course, most children growing up in ancient Egypt didn't have all that Moses had; he was a wealthy, privileged kid.

As he moved on into his teens, his twenties, even into his thirties, he became known for four distinguishing characteristics. The first, which even historians took note of, was how good-looking Moses was. Dr. Gene Getz, in his book *Moses: Moments of Glory . . . Feet of Clay*, notes that Moses was so physically outstanding that the Egyptians would often stare at him, finding it hard to turn their eyes away from such an unusual young man.[iii] Being the son of Pharaoh's daughter and the only apparent heir to the king's throne, of course, made this even more intriguing.

The second thing you would notice about Moses is that he was highly educated. As I said, Egypt was quite advanced—in architecture, engineering, art and mathematics. The nation's social, economic and educational achievements were almost unprecedented. The pyramids, for example, reflect mathematical insights, artistic skill and feats of engineering that are almost inconceivable for a culture that existed so many years ago.

It is logical, therefore, to conclude that Moses probably became one of the most educated young men in the world. Gene Getz puts it this way: "With free tuition, personalized instruction from the best scholars in the land and an eager and aspiring young mind, Moses was destined to receive his Ph.D. from the University of Egypt, graduating summa cum laude."[iv]

On looks and brains alone, Moses could have run for Mr. Egypt and won it hands down. But that's not all. There's a third thing you would have noticed about him: He had great leadership skills. We get a hint of that in Acts 7:22, where Stephen says that Moses "was mighty in his words and deeds." But we see it clearly in the works of the historian Josephus, who records that when the Ethiopians rose up against the Egyptians, Pharaoh called on Moses to raise up an army and protect Egypt. And the story goes that Moses not only defeated the Ethiopians, but in such a strategic, ingenious way that he became a hero in all of Egypt. [v] What an accomplished guy!

And there's a fourth thing. Not only was he good-looking, educated and a great leader, he was also very wealthy. If you were Moses, your typical morning probably went something like this: You are sleeping in a luxurious bed, covered with the finest linens in the world. As you wake up and drop your feet on the floor, they come to rest on costly tile that's been hand-laid. You get up and walk over to your chest of drawers, made of the choicest wood in the land. Hanging in your closet are the finest clothes ever known to mankind.

You're hungry, so you step into your dining room and legions of servants are falling all over themselves, asking what you would like. Do you want bacon and eggs this morning? They are placed before you in a flash. Changed your mind? No problem! They'll throw the bacon and eggs to the dogs and make you cornflakes, or anything you want. That's how Moses grew up—a very privileged upbringing.

And yet, even with these great qualities and privileges, there was a single haunting question in Moses' mind that kept surfacing over and over again, that kept him awake at night, until he couldn't find rest in his soul or peace in his heart. Everything in life seemed to lose its meaning until nothing mattered anymore but the answer to this question: *What am I living for?*

Isn't that amazing? Moses—with all his wealth, prestige and education—struggled with the very same mystery you and I are trying to figure out: *How do I make sense of my life? What difference does it make? Who am I? What am I here for?* It seems that no matter how much we have, no matter how privileged we are, no matter how educated, we all come to the same burning question: *What's my purpose in life?*

You don't have to look very hard to see that nature has a purposeful design. That's because God is a very purposeful God. It doesn't take long to figure out that there might be a purpose for you being here. It doesn't take much intelligence or education to think about that. And Moses was thinking about that, haunted by that, trying to discover that. Finally, he came to a conclusion—the same conclusion you and I need to come to: If we're going to find meaning in life, if we're going to find God, we have to seek purpose over comfort. I know that because of what it says in Hebrews 11:24–26:

> By faith Moses, when he was grown up, refused to be
> called the son of Pharaoh's daughter, choosing rather to

be mistreated with the people of God than to enjoy the fleeting pleasures of sin. He considered the reproach of Christ greater wealth than the treasures of Egypt, for he was looking to the reward.

It's easy for us to read a passage like that in the comfort of an air-conditioned building and a cushy chair and totally miss the point. Just like us, Moses struggled to make sense of his life. And he came to the conclusion that he was never going to find real meaning in his life by seeking his own comfort. He would have to seek the purpose that God designed him for. This is a tough choice—and the same one you and I need to make. Let's see how it unfolds in various areas of life, through the example of Moses.

IN YOUR FAMILY

Hebrews 11:24 tells us that "By faith Moses, when he was grown up, refused to be called the son of Pharaoh's daughter." Do you seek God's purpose over comfort in your family? That must have been a question that came to Moses' mind. And as you can see, he came up with an answer. But imagine the struggle, the emotional turmoil, the frustration! He must have felt a great sense of obligation to Pharaoh's daughter, the woman he probably called "Mom."

But she was not his real mother. And by deciding not to be called her son anymore, he rejected all the prestige, the education, the privilege, the material things that came with that role. He may have even been rejecting the future throne of Egypt.

How do you think Pharaoh's daughter found out? Maybe she heard rumors of it before she heard it from him. But there must have come a day of confrontation when he said to her, "I can't go on like this. I can't be called your son anymore. It's not true—you know it's not true."

Imagine how she felt. I'm sure she said something like, "Oh, you don't really mean that, Moses! After I've loved you and taken care of you for so many years? After all I've given you—all the honor and privileges and gifts? Would you give up all that?" And he must have replied, "Don't you understand? It means nothing to me anymore."

What led him to make that life-altering decision? Was it the result of paying a visit to Jochebed? Or was it seeing the daily torture and torment of his own people? Could it be that he heard the voice of God pricking his conscience? I don't know. But somehow he answered the cry for meaning and purpose in his life—the same cry each one of us has. And he realized it would mean turning away from a life of lies, even if it meant giving up privilege and prestige and facing the rejection of the only family he had ever known.

But what if he hadn't made that decision? What if he had decided to just go along with it and try to find purpose and meaning in being the son of Pharaoh's daughter? I'm sure that someone in Pharaoh's household would have taken him aside and said, "Hey, aren't you getting into this religion stuff a little too far? It's great that you want to find meaning in your life, but come on, Moses! Don't you get it? You can be pharaoh someday! You're just going through a phase; you'll get over it." Isn't it helpful to have friends and relatives like that, to lead you astray with their great advice? It still happens today.

A little book by Maurice Wagner, *The Sensation of Being Somebody,* sums up what Moses was struggling with. Wagner says, "We've developed several equations for our sense of being a somebody. But none of them really balance in our lives. For example, some believe that appearance plus admiration equals a whole person. It's all about looking really good." [vi]

Well, Moses did look really good. And he was certainly admired; he was like a hero in the land. Did it make him a whole person? No, he decided. And if you base your life on that, you'll come to the same conclusion.

Wagner identifies another equation many follow: Performance plus accomplishments equals a whole person.[vii] If I can be the best at what I do, that will really make me somebody. Well, Moses was the best; after all, he conquered the Ethiopians. He was tough. He was accomplished. But it didn't matter. It didn't make him a whole person.

Another equation that's often followed is status plus recognition equals a whole person. Did Moses have that? Absolutely! Did it make him a whole person? No, he still struggled with the same question you and I struggle with: *What's my life all about?* Wagner comments,

> Try as we might by our appearance, our performance and our social status to find self-verification for a sense of being somebody, we always come short of satisfaction. Whatever pinnacle of self-identity we achieve soon crumbles under the pressures of hostile rejection or criticism, introspection or guilt, fear and anxiety. [viii]

Hopefully in your life you have begun to come to know the only real equation that makes life make sense: God plus you equals a whole person. If you try to find yourself without finding Him as well, you'll always find nothing, nothing but yourself. That's the very reason you're searching so hard: At the core of truly understanding who you are is knowing God.

God is the only one who can bring true purpose into your life. Meaning: That's what Moses discovered. And if he had not done this, I wonder what would have happened? He wouldn't have been the one to deliver the Hebrew people from Egypt, would he?

Could there be a purpose in your life that you're missing because you won't make the right choice—you won't choose purpose over comfort? Will God have to find someone else to do the job?

IN YOUR FRIENDSHIPS

The book of Hebrews also says that Moses chose "rather to be mistreated with the people of God than to enjoy the fleeting pleasures of sin" (11:25). When I read that, I see two groups of friends—one that says life is all about being comfortable and having a good time, and another that says life is all about honoring God and having purpose and meaning. It's a choice of friendships, isn't it? Moses chose to identify with the people of God rather than all the comforts and luxuries he could have, because he couldn't find meaning in pleasure. Do you seek God's purpose over comfort in your friendships?

Many people claim to be Christians, yet their friendships tell another story; if they were really identifying with God, how could they be friends with such people? I'm not saying that you can't have a friend who's not a believer. Of course you can, and you should. But are most of your friends, especially your closest and most influential friends, outside the kingdom? Your close friendships reveal your true loyalties. Moses realized this, so he made a hard decision. He knew that if he wanted to find meaning and purpose in his life, he would have to identify with the people of God.

In 1987 I was asked to speak at a local high school on the subject of sex. It was an honor to be able to give a biblical perspective to these kids. And they listened closely; for many of them, what I was saying was radical to their ears. I knew, of course, that they would probably be too embarrassed to talk with me after class, so I wrote my phone number on the board and said, "If any of you has questions or would like to talk with me sometime, just give me a call."

You'd be surprised how many called me. I remember one fifteen-year-old girl called and told me about the situation she found herself in. She and her eighteen-year-old boyfriend were having sex on a regular basis. She asked me, "Do you really believe that you shouldn't have sex until you're married?" I went on to explain to her why I believed that to be so, why I believed it was the healthiest choice—physically, emotionally and spiritually.

She replied, "But I won't have any boyfriends; all my friends will think I'm strange."

I said, "Well, you have a choice to make, don't you? Are you going to live for purpose or for pleasure?" It's the same choice we all have to make. One has meaning, one doesn't.

DO YOU SEEK GOD'S PURPOSE ABOVE ALL?

Hebrews 11:26 reveals that Moses made a third decision, as well: "He considered the reproach of Christ greater wealth than the treasures of Egypt, for he was looking to the reward." He turned away from the luxury, prestige, money, fame, education—all the things he had as the top dog in the top country in the world—and became associated with the Hebrew people and the Hebrew God, because he thought it was of greater value. He had everything he could humanly want, yet he said, "I found something better."

What could that "something better" be? If you've got everything in the world, then it has to be something out of this world. And it was—it was God. That's what Moses found. When you find a relationship with God, you find deeper riches than anyone could find in this world. If you can't understand that kind of thinking, it's because you have not made the kind of decisions Moses made or understood the kind of God Moses had. You don't know Him.

I can relate to what Moses is saying. I've experienced some of the same things myself. Understanding and knowing God is greater than any pleasure you can have here in this world. Moses grabbed hold of that. Even though he had it all—more than you or I will ever have—he decided it was of greater value to know God. That's a powerful statement.

I've observed that Christians who live as Christians suffer no matter where they live. For example, I've never resided in a country where preaching the gospel was illegal or where I would have to fear imprisonment for my preaching. But, I have been mocked, belittled, teased and made fun of for sharing my faith. I've experienced the hurt that comes when people I trusted have disappointed me or even betrayed me. I've also had others disregard my needs after I have spent countless hours tending to their needs.

I have come to realize that no matter who you are or how "nice" you may be, if you are a Christian living as a Christian should, you will suffer. At that point, when you have encountered the suffering inherent in the life of a Christian, you have a choice. You could easily try to avoid situations that may lead to hurt by deciding not to commit to helping others. Many Christians have wrongfully done that. Or, you could decide it is no longer safe to trust others so deeply. Or you could just separate yourself from others and say, "Others are not my responsibility at all. I'll take care of myself and they will have to deal with themselves."

Many have either consciously or unconsciously made such decisions and have literally cut themselves off from knowing God any deeper. By trying to cut out suffering in our lives we will always cut out God.

Also, by trying to avoid suffering, we become disobedient to God's will. In other words, there comes a point in everyone's life where a decision has to be made to live for purpose or for comfort. And I believe our churches are full of people who have chosen comfort. They say they're Christians, but their values, friendships and families reveal that they're living for pleasure.

How about you? Maybe you need to change like Moses changed and start living for purpose over pleasure. You won't find satisfaction and fulfillment in life if, in your family, friendships and values, you are choosing pleasure and comfort over and over again.

Could God have a purpose for letting you live in the richest country in the world? Is there a purpose for you being one of the most educated people in the world? (Even if you only have a high school diploma, you're far more educated than most people in the world.) God has a grand plan and a purpose, and just like Moses, you've been put in a very strategic place. Don't miss the opportunity.

In the book *Halftime*, Bob Buford tells how, as the CEO of his own company in his forties, he began asking himself questions, just like a modern-day Moses. He had come to a point in life he calls "halftime"—the midway point—and he was beginning to wonder how he should live the second half. In the first half of life he had been very successful. But he decided he wanted more than success in the second half; he wanted to do something significant.

Ironically, God showed him the solution to his dilemma through the words of a friend, a business consultant who was not even a believer. After he shared his struggles, his friend asked, "Bob, what's in your box? You know, if you open up a clock, you'll find a mainspring inside; you wind it up and it runs the whole machine. What's your mainspring? What's driving you? What are you excited about? What do you want to become? You tell me what's in your box, and I can give you a plan." [ix]

Bob explained that he was looking for a new way to live out his Christian convictions and was serious about shifting at least some of his energies away from business pursuits into some unspecified realm of service.

His answer didn't satisfy his friend, because he replied, "I'm gonna ask you again: What's in your box? For you, it is either money or Jesus Christ. If you can tell me which it is, I can tell you the strategic plan you need to implement. If you can't tell me what it is, you're going to oscillate between those two decisions the rest of your life."[x]

No one had ever stated the issue that clearly to Bob before. He realized he would never do anything significant or know the purpose God had for him, until he decided. So he said, "I put Jesus Christ in the box." It was the best decision he ever made. He went on to start a ministry called Leadership Network, which has had a profound impact in the United States But it never would have happened if he hadn't answered his friend's question, "What's in your box?"

Let me ask you: What's in your box? Have you made the decision between purpose and comfort?

Chapter 4

How to Keep from Going Wrong

When you choose comfort over purpose, you're likely to find that you end up with neither comfort nor purpose. Life goes wrong when you make wrong decisions. It's that simple. As Moses' story continues in Exodus 2, we learn how he went wrong. I believe this passage of Scripture is here as a warning for us. God opens up Moses' life for us to say, "Your life will go wrong too if you make the same kind of wrong decisions, but you can avoid that." That's what revelation is all about. God reveals to us truth so we can avoid making wrong decisions.

A little over twenty years ago I was sitting in class at seminary when one of the professors walked in, obviously very upset. "Something is really going wrong here," he said. "We teach, train and mentor, we do everything we possibly can, yet there are students who leave this school after years of training and fall down in the ministry. What are we doing wrong? What aren't we doing? Would you clue me in?" This professor was opening his heart. He was hurting, and we all knew what he was talking about.

The story had come out about a student who had graduated a few years before. A former professional football player, he left that career, enrolled at the seminary and became a top student. Then, after a few years in ministry, he left his wife, shacked up with another woman and was now doing some secular job. And our professor was asking, "What happened? How did his life go so wrong?"

What that professor was talking about that morning is the same thing we see in Exodus 2:11–15. Moses had been doing quite well. He was raised in a palace. He was good-looking, well-educated, a gifted leader and very, very wealthy. But in Hebrews 11 we learn that Moses had come to a decision in his life not to be called the son of Pharaoh's daughter, but to be known as a Hebrew, a child of Yahweh. He decided to follow the God of his people and that led to a lot of changes.

Change—isn't it something? Change happens in everybody's life. Don't you sometimes want to just kind of put your life on pause and freeze it right there? Things are going great, so you don't want anything to change. And at other times, you're hoping something changes soon, because you can't stand it anymore! It's kind of a love-hate thing with change, isn't it?

Well, Moses dealt with the same thing in his life, and the changes were significant. The pharaoh, whose daughter had found him in the Nile, died; a new pharaoh, who saw Moses as a threat, took over in Egypt. But the most significant change that occurred was in Moses' heart. He now wanted to be connected with the Hebrew people. One day he went for a walk to watch them at their work. He was appalled when he saw the heartache, the pain, the ruthless treatment they received at the hands of the Egyptians, and he felt called by God to do something about it.

With these thoughts in his mind, he suddenly came upon an arrogant, obnoxious Egyptian ruthlessly beating a Hebrew slave. He probably cried out, "Hey! What are you doing?! Leave him alone!" I'm sure the Egyptian looked at him with a sneer and just laughed, then went on kicking and beating the poor man.

Rage took over Moses' heart. Have you ever watched a movie with a really mean villain, and you just can't wait for the part where the bad guy gets his comeuppance? Multiply that about ten times and you'll have an idea of how Moses probably felt. I can do something about this, he thought, so he did. He looked to see if anybody was watching, then grabbed the Egyptian and killed him. That's how much rage he had. He felt like justice had been served. Then he buried the body in the sand and went away thinking he had committed the perfect murder: No one saw; no one knew. Besides, the guy had it coming. That's what Moses was thinking—until the next day.

He went for another walk, still trying to relate to his people, trying to figure out how to make a difference, and saw two Hebrew slaves fighting with one another. He picked out the guy he thought was in the wrong and said, "Hey, leave him alone; don't we have enough problems dealing with the Egyptians? We've got to stick together. We can't go beating on each other."

This guy looked Moses in the face and probably said something like, "Who do you think you are? Who died and made you a ruler over me? In fact, I heard yesterday that you beat an Egyptian to death. You took care of your problem, and I'm taking care of mine; get out of my face."

Moses was hurt that they wouldn't respond to him, but even more, he was shocked to learn that someone had found out what he had done. I'm in trouble here, he thought. This is going to get back to Pharaoh. Sure enough, Moses' fears were justified: It did get back to the pharaoh, who sent out a posse to kill him. So Moses ran away, the Scriptures tell us, to a place called Midian, on the east shore of the Sinai Peninsula. When he got there, he sat down by a well.

"WHERE DID I GO WRONG?"

Imagine how Moses must have felt. There he was, just
trying to serve God, just trying to do what he felt he was
called to do—deliver his people—and then he became a
fugitive from justice, sitting by a well in a foreign land. He
had no clothes—and he used to wear the finest clothes in the
land. He had no food—and he used to eat nothing but the
finest food known to mankind. He had no place to live—and
he used to live in a palace. Moses was depressed, confused,
totally bewildered. "Lord, what are you doing to me? Where
did I go wrong?"

Have you ever been there? We all have—even people
who know God, like Moses, still get there sometimes. We're
confused, bewildered, feeling like everything has gone wrong.
But in this story the reason is only too clear: It all went wrong
because Moses made a wrong decision.

As I said, I believe God revealed this story in Scripture
for our benefit. He opened up Moses' life for you and me,
thousands of years later, so we can avoid making the mistakes
he did. You can avoid making wrong decisions and keep your
life from going wrong if you learn two lessons from this story.

The first is this: You make wrong decisions when you
make them alone. Notice in the story that Moses never once
consulted anyone else. He had no friend to talk to, no one
else to debate this with. Wouldn't it have been great if he had
somebody to say, "Moses, how is murdering this guy going to
deliver your people? What are you going to do—kill all the
Egyptians one at a time? Come on, this is a stupid idea!"

He needed someone to question him, to help him think
through his actions. But he wasn't calling on anyone else for
advice. He wasn't teamed up with his people enough to be able
to talk things through with them. He was going at things the
wrong way by going it alone.

This story points out the importance of having a Christian friend in your life—someone who listens to God and with whom you can discuss things. Unfortunately, many people, even in church, don't ever do that. They make major decisions—where to live, where to work, who to spend their lives with—and they never ask anyone for input. If you do that, you are heading for big mistakes; it puts you in a very vulnerable position. It's very important to bring others in on your decisions—and I'm not just talking about consulting other humans; I'm talking about consulting God.

Notice in the story that you never see Moses praying to God, *Please show me, Lord, how You want me to rescue Your people from oppression in Egypt.* It is critical that we make decisions with the Lord, not just for the Lord. Moses had it right that he was called by God to rescue the children of Israel from oppression in Egypt. He just went about it his own way, doing what seemed right to him. I'm afraid that many times we do exactly the same thing. Why is that?

In Moses' case, it may have been because he was so handsome, educated and rich. He was used to getting things done, to having people listen to him and respect him. That describes a lot of us as well: We make good money; we have influence; we know how to make things happen. That puts us in a risky place—we are tempted to just make decisions ourselves, because we can.

We need to realize how much we need the Lord, as well as a good friend or spouse, to question us and make us think through what we are doing. Sometimes I wonder if the major thing wrong with the American church, and the reason Christianity is going down in America while in other countries it is going up, is because American Christians are wealthy, educated and handsome! Is it because we are so confident in ourselves that we don't turn to God? Could we be repeating the same dumb mistake Moses made?

In my many years as a Christian, I have seen some of the dumbest, stupidest things done by the most educated and smartest people I have ever met. They may be educated, but they don't have common sense. Perhaps it's because they have been told all their lives that they are smart, so they say to themselves, "I'm smart enough that I don't need to question what I'm thinking. I don't need to have anyone else question me. In fact, I don't even need to ask the Lord." That's a dangerous way of thinking. Maybe that was Moses' problem.

Someone recently gave me a new pen. It's the nicest one I have—though I probably won't have it for long, because I'll lose it! A pen is made for a purpose; no matter how expensive it is or how nice it looks, it's still a pen and it's made for writing. A pen lying flat in my hand is useless for what it was created to do, isn't it? It was made for writing, but it can't write lying on its side. The only way it can fulfill the purpose for which it was created is if it is taken up and put on its end. Then it can write out a message.

In the same way, God created you and me; He called us to Himself just as He called Moses. Every Christian is called to Him for a purpose, given a gift and a job to do. There's a life message He wants you to write out, but it's not going to happen unless you're picked up and put on your end. Your message can only come out when God's holding you up.

Often, your friends can hold you up—those you listen to, the people who influence you. But as we all know, friends can let you down; they are just people. Certainly, God can use friends in our lives—that's why He's given us the church, the body of Christ—but our relationship with God is the only thing that can hold us up so that we can write out the message He wants to communicate to this world through us. He had a message to communicate through Moses, but Moses was like a pen trying to write by itself. It didn't work.

God went on to teach Moses through this Midian experience. He went to school for forty years—God's school this time, not the Egyptians'. He got trained on how to have a relationship with God and began to realize how desperately he needed to follow God step-by-step. When he learned to let God hold him up and hold together his life, then he could write out the message God had to communicate through him.

It's true for me, for you and for everyone who is called to God through Jesus Christ. There is a message you are supposed to communicate to your kids, your church, your community, your country; there is a purpose for you. You'll never know it; you'll never fulfill it; you'll get it all wrong unless you go to God for guidance. You want to make right decisions? Don't do it alone. Make sure you are connecting with God. Get renewed; pray, talk with him, listen.

The second lesson we learn from this passage is this: You make wrong decisions when you are not being honest. Look at Exodus 2:12: "He looked this way and that, and seeing no one, he struck down the Egyptian and hid him in the sand." What do people do right before they cheat on a test or take something that doesn't belong to them? They look this way and that. Then they pull out the crib sheet or slip that item in their pockets. It's a sign that they are not being honest. Moses was not being honest—not with God, with himself or with those who might be watching him (and obviously someone was!).

We've seen how important honesty is in recent history. Two American Presidents—Richard Nixon and Bill Clinton—both made this kind of mistake. They weren't honest with themselves, with the people they served or with God. As a result, they made really wrong decisions—stupid, hurtful, character-destroying decisions—because their characters were already dishonest. Eventually, their dishonesty was brought into the public spotlight.

A business consultant I know says that one thing he has learned in his work is that if you don't deal with the issues in your life privately—issues such as dishonesty—someday you will have to deal with them in a public forum. Isn't that exactly what happened with Bill Clinton and Richard Nixon? And it's exactly what happened with Moses. He wasn't dealing with his dishonesty privately, so it became a public thing; everybody knew.

He soon discovered just how public it had become:

> When he went out the next day, behold, two Hebrews were struggling together. And he said to the man in the wrong, "Why do you strike your companion?"
>
> He answered, "Who made you a prince and a judge over us? Do you mean to kill me as you killed the Egyptian?" (Exod. 2:13–14)

Why this reaction? After all, this was Moses, the hope of the Hebrew people! He's handsome and educated, and he's coming down to their level, trying to help them out. How come all of a sudden this guy has no respect for him? It's because he sees the dishonesty in Moses' life. It's as if he were saying, "You manipulate, cheat and lie to get what you want, like anybody else. You're no different from us; why should I follow you?"

This is true in any leadership position. Parents, for example, know how true it is with their kids. Often in their teen years, when you're saying, "Don't do this, do that," they look you in the eye and say, "Who made you ruler and judge over me?" Why do they say that? Why do they lose respect for you so fast? Could it be they see the dishonesty in your life?

A book I read not long ago on child rearing said that is exactly what goes on. That's why raising teenagers is so tough; they know your stuff and they throw it right back at you. Sure, they might be trying to manipulate you, but the point is, have they caught you being dishonest? When they catch you, have you said, "I'm sorry, please forgive me"?

Wouldn't it have been wonderful if Richard Nixon and Bill Clinton had gone on public TV and confessed to the whole nation, "I was dead wrong; it's all my fault. Please forgive me"? We could have respected them again. But they didn't. Moses played the same kind of game, and people won't follow a leader like that. God was calling him to be a leader, but you can't lead and not be honest, openhearted and truthful. You can't lead and cover up sin.

With our children sometimes this truth hits us in the face. But we see it in the workplace, at church and in our relationships as well. Let's face it, all of us have blind spots—ways we are not being honest even with ourselves. Thank God He brings people into our lives—even, perhaps, someone as obnoxious and rude as the Hebrew Moses encountered—to help us see the truth about ourselves.

If you don't have a clear conscience before God and before men, I guarantee you're going to make some very wrong decisions in your life—decisions that will probably be very hurtful to you and to those you love. So you need to be dead sure you are being honest with those you love and not being manipulative—that you're not trying to promote something or make something happen just for yourself. We see it pretty clearly in the lives of those Presidents, as well as in the life of Moses. Honesty is very, very important.

When I was in my early twenties, I was seeking God's will for my life—what kind of work He wanted me to do, if I should be in ministry and all of those kinds of things. Then I heard a speaker say something that has influenced me ever since: "God is not as concerned with what you do as how you do what you do."

Moses knew he was called by God to deliver the children of Israel, but he was going about it all wrong. God wants a day-by-day, minute-by-minute personal relationship with you, in which you seek Him about your decisions, talk with Him and relate to Him in the how-tos of life. If He told you everything He wanted you to do, all at once, you wouldn't need to communicate with Him; you wouldn't need a relationship. But God told Moses plague by plague what to do; He didn't tell him about all ten plagues at once. In a living, active relationship with God, Moses learned how to deliver the children of Israel from Egypt—one of the greatest feats in human history.

How are you going to do what you're supposed to do? How are you going to be a good spouse, a better parent? How are you going to fulfill what God is calling you to do in your church, in the ministry He's given you? Get away with God and talk with Him. Just as He did with Moses, He will show you, day by day, moment by moment.

Chapter 5

FINDING GOD'S POWER FOR YOUR LIFE

A while ago I talked with a very disillusioned Christian. Over lunch he shared with me the details of his dilemma—the sicknesses plaguing him and those he loved, the problems and frustrations that threatened to overwhelm him. Trying to relate to his feelings, I said, "Well, I guess you feel like God's really being silent right now."

"No, it's worse than that," he replied.

"OK," I suggested, "you not only feel like He's not talking to you, but you also feel like your prayers don't go past the ceiling, like He's not helping you, right?"

"No, it's worse than that, Marty," he answered in a bitter tone. "I feel like God's against me. He's not only silent; He's not only not helping me; I feel like He's actually working against me."

Do you think maybe that's how Moses felt when he was sitting by the well in Midian, on the run from an Egyptian posse? I think that's exactly how he felt. "Lord, I'm trying to do what You want me to do—free the people of Israel from slavery in Egypt—and You're working against me here." Have you ever felt like that?

Everyone needs to get to the place where they say, "I can't do this," because it's true—you can't! You need the power of God, just like Moses did. Nobody serves God without God's power. He doesn't need your power. He wants you to be an instrument of His power. That's what Moses began to grab onto here.

Though we may hate to admit it, we all feel powerless sometimes. Maybe there's an addiction in your life that you feel powerless against. Maybe you feel powerless in your relationship with your spouse, your parents or your children; perhaps you feel powerless at work or in your finances. Is there anything in your life that makes you feel powerless? That's not a bad place to be, because you can learn to draw on the power of God.

Moses was in the same place we are: He was powerless. As we look at his story and how it unfolds, we can see three principles he learned for drawing on God's power. I'm not talking about some kind of "magic formula" that you put into effect to somehow gain God's power, but three principles which, if you learn and apply them, can bring the same results that Moses saw. You can see God at work in your life.

We left Moses in the last chapter at Exodus 2:15, sitting by the well in Midian. Picture the scene: he comes to the well after walking for days. As far as we know, he has nothing but the clothes on his back. He had to leave town in a hurry, because Pharaoh was out to kill him; he's a wanted man, with no supplies or food. It must be tough for a guy who is used to the luxury of a palace to find himself without anything.

Moses dropped the bucket in the well to get a drink, walked over to the shade of a tree and just sat there. He was discouraged, disillusioned, in a daze. Maybe you've been there. After taking a few sips of water, he probably began thinking, *Now what do I do? I'm stuck out here in the middle of nowhere. The sign says this is Midian. Where in the world is that?*

He saw a flock of sheep coming toward the well, led by some shepherds—but they didn't look like shepherds. As they got closer, he realized they were women—seven women—walking along, talking and tending the sheep. They didn't even notice Moses; they just walked up to the well and began to water their sheep. Moses was probably not in a very friendly mood at that point, so he just sat and watched.

Suddenly, out of nowhere came another flock of sheep, with some shepherds herding it. The shepherds barged right in and started grabbing the bucket from the women, saying, "Sorry girls, you're going to have to move out of the way; we're serious shepherds and we've got a job to do."

Moses wasn't in a very good mood anyway, but when he saw this happen, it really ticked him off. This just wasn't right. Moses had a thing about justice: He couldn't stand to see someone being treated unfairly. So he walked over to these shepherds and said, "Hey, buddy, I believe that bucket belongs to her. You need to get in line and wait your turn. Hand me that bucket."

I'm sure there was a tense moment there, but as far as we know, there was no fight. They handed him the bucket and he said, "Thank you. I think I'll help these young ladies water their sheep." Imagine what these girls were thinking after this good-looking guy rescued them from those bullies! They hurried home because they couldn't wait to tell their father.

"How come you're back so soon?" he asked.

"When we went to the well to water the sheep, these shepherds started pushing us around and grabbing our water," they said. "But then this Egyptian came along and scared them off. He even watered the sheep for us."

"Well, where is he?" Reuel asked. And they said, "He's back at the well."

"What? You mean you didn't bring him home? What's wrong with you girls? Didn't I teach you any manners?" their father cried. "Go back to the well and get him. This is the kind of guy I need around here."

So he sent the girls back to find Moses and bring him back to the house—which I'm sure they were only too happy to do! And they invited him to dinner, which was a customary courtesy to strangers in those days.

As they ate together, Reuel (also known as Jethro) started telling Moses that he was a Midianite—a descendant of Midian, the son of Keturah by Abraham. Moses said, "I'm a descendant of Abraham too. I know I'm dressed like an Egyptian, but I'm a Jew—we're relatives!" This made things even more interesting. Soon they had developed a relationship, and Jethro invited Moses to stay with them. Eventually, Moses married Zipporah, one of Jethro's daughters, and lived there in Midian for forty years (see Exod. 2:16–22).

THE BURNING BUSH

Moses was now living a totally different life—tending sheep, learning about farming, being a family man and living as part of a clan. Since Jethro, his father-in-law, was a priest of Yahweh, Moses was also learning about God in a whole new dimension. He couldn't have learned those things back in the palace in Egypt. He was learning how to worship and honor God and probably how to live with God in a personal relationship.

One day, Moses was out with the sheep on the back side of the property, by a mountain called Horeb, which was known as "the mountain of God." Looking up the hill, he saw a fire. *That's strange,* he thought. *Oh, well, maybe some nomads left their campfire burning.* So he turned his attention back to the sheep.

A couple of hours later, he looked and saw that the fire was still burning. This started to bother him, so he left the sheep to check it out. As he got closer, he said to himself, "It looks like a burning bush; why hasn't it burned out?" Once he got near the bush, he heard a voice from within it call out, "Moses!"

He had never heard a bush talk before! But when the voice said, "Moses!" to him again, he replied, "Here I am!" And the voice said, "Take your sandals off your feet, for the place on which you are standing is holy ground" (Exod. 3:5). As he quickly took his shoes off, he said, "Who are you?"

"I am ... the God of Abraham, ... Isaac and ... Jacob" (3:6).

If I were Moses, I would probably be thinking, *Oh no, He's here to talk to me about killing that Egyptian!* Isn't that the first thing you'd think about? *Oh boy, I'm in big trouble.* But instead, God basically said, "Moses, I've heard the cry of My people in their distress, and I want to bring them into a land flowing with milk and honey. Moses, I'm sending you to Pharaoh, to deliver My people from slavery in Egypt" (see Exodus 3:7–10).

Let's look at some principles from Moses' encounter with God that can help us in our lives as Christians.

1. LIVE WITH GOD IN THE NOW

The first is this: God's power is found by learning to be with God right now. Notice that nowhere in this story does God mention Moses' past. Don't you find that a little peculiar? He murdered someone—and God doesn't even bring it up? No, God lets it go. I think it was because Moses had learned how to be with God. He had learned how to seek God and be forgiven by Him. His father-in-law had taught him to seek God with all his heart.

If you have some failure in your past—maybe a moral failure, maybe an act of denial like Peter—you can take hope. Look how greatly God used Peter, who denied his Lord. Look how greatly God used Moses, who had murdered a man and looked at his past as a total failure. God just said, "It doesn't matter; if you're ready, I'm ready. I want to use you."

I believe God is saying that to everyone today just as much as He did to Moses. He's saying, "My power is going to be available to you if you can learn to live with Me right now." That's what Moses had learned. He had learned how to live with God—while having a wife, a family and a job.

Do you want to learn to get the power of God? Start with your marriage and your kids. Start with the job you've got right now—not the job you're someday going to get. We so often want to think about the future and forget about right now. The secret to getting God's power in your life is to start now—right now, with what's bothering you today, the situation you're in today. This is extremely important. It can't be emphasized enough.

2. PAY ATTENTION TO GOD'S WORK

The second principle we learn from Moses' encounter with God is this: God's power is found by paying attention to His work. Why did God have a bush that burned and didn't burn out? There's only one reason—to get Moses' attention. And when He had Moses' attention, He could speak to Moses' heart.

Is there a "burning bush" in your life—a singular situation, whether good or bad? Maybe you just got a raise or a promotion. Maybe you're getting married or going to have a baby. Maybe you've received a bad report from the doctor. Or maybe you didn't get a raise, but a cut in salary. It could be good fortune or bad fortune, but it's a burning bush. It's something that gets you to ask, just as Moses did when he was walking up the hill toward that bush, "What is going on here? What is this all about?" It gets your attention.

When these things happen, you can respond in one of two ways. You can focus all your attention on the bush, or you can ask yourself the question, "What does God have to say to me through this?"

I am amazed at how many people I see with burning bushes in their lives. It is so obvious that God is trying to say something to them, but all they're doing is wondering why the bush is burning! "Why is this going on? I can't understand why this would happen to me!" Hey, listen up! God is trying to get your attention here. One of the main reasons God lets these things happen is to get our attention. Ask God, "What do I need to hear? Speak to me through this burning bush." It might be a trial, it might be suffering, but you've got to listen. Someone once said, "God screams to us through our pain." It's our burning bush.

I believe very firmly that the burning World Trade Center towers and Pentagon on September 11, 2001, were like God's burning bush to America. Just as God got Moses' attention through a burning bush, I think God is speaking to America. I feel that He is calling us to action. Now, I don't expect all Americans to hear His voice through this, but I do expect believers to hear. I am hoping that this event in our history, as well as the many that have come since then, helps the church turn around. We need to listen very clearly to what God is saying.

The disillusioned Christian I mentioned at the beginning of this chapter told me at one point in our conversation, "I feel like I need to be filled with the Spirit." I agreed with him; being filled with the Spirit means being controlled by God's Spirit, not by yourself. But then he said, "You know, sometimes in worship the Lord touches your heart and speaks to you in a powerful way. That's what I need—one of those anointed times, one of those touches from the Lord."

I felt like responding, "Hey, pal, wake up! All these problems in your life—don't you understand you've got a burning bush here? God is ready to speak to you, much more than through some church service or spiritual experience—as legitimate as those things are. You can be filled with the Spirit by yielding to God right now and listening, rather than by having some experience."

Sometimes as Christians we're guilty of looking for some exceptional thing happening instead of asking ourselves, "What's happening right now? Is there a bush right here?" Was Moses looking for something spectacular? No, he was just going along in his life, tending the sheep, when boom!— there's a bush! The same thing happens today. You're just going along, doing your job, taking care of the kids and— boom!—there's a bush! That's the way God speaks. He'll use something in your life, maybe even push your buttons, to get your attention.

And God knows how to do it. He knows you, and He knows how to get your attention. You just need to pay attention. To get God's power into your life, to be able to grab hold of it like Moses did, you've got to wake up and listen to what God has to say to you in those burning bushes.

3. OBEY GOD

The third principle we learn from Moses is in Exodus 3:10: "So now, go. I am sending you to Pharaoh to bring my people the Israelites out of Egypt" (NIV). In my Bible I circled the word go. To see God's power in your life, you need to do more than live with God in the now and listen to burning bushes. You also have to obey everything God tells you. And if you are a Christian, God has told you to go.

Jesus said in Matthew 28:19, "Go therefore and make disciples of all nations." If you're wondering why you don't see the power of God in your life like other Christians do, could it be because you've never gone—never gone to your friend, your neighbor, your relatives? Until you obey what He told you, you're never going to experience His power.

Many Christians say, "Bless me, Lord! Bless me, Lord!" But they're not going anywhere. If Moses had asked for a blessing, God would have responded, "Bless you? For what? You haven't done what I told you to do—go! Millions of people are back in Egypt suffering; they're crying every day. Your brothers and sisters, Moses, are enslaved back in Egypt!"

Millions of people have not heard the gospel yet. Thousands of people in your area don't know about Christ. They don't know how to make Jesus Christ their Master, to grow into maturity and develop their mission in life. We're called to go. And to truly experience God's power in your life, somehow, some way, you need to pursue that cause—through the ministry you're involved in, through your personal contacts with friends and neighbors. Then you'll start to see the power of God in your life and experience Him like you're supposed to. To have God's power you need to obey.

Moses was pretty comfortable in Midian; he had a wife and kids, and everything was going along fine. Then God said, "Go back to Egypt," and Moses said, "I don't think so; they don't really like me back there." In the next chapter, we'll see how he argued with God about that. I'm afraid that you and I often do the same thing.

The good news is Moses did go. And once he started to go, God told him more of the plan. God may not tell you everything that He wants you to do, but when you pick up and say, "OK, I'm making a commitment to go," that's step one. He'll show you the next step.

Chapter 6

God's Deliverance Can Happen

As we saw in the last chapter, the first step in answering God's call is surrendering your heart. Surrender, however, is not easy. Most of us go through some kind of struggle, and the story of Moses at the burning bush was no exception.

What do you do when you are facing a burning bush in your life? Well, you can run. Moses could have done that—after all, he must have been ashamed of how his life had turned out. Exodus 3:6 says that he turned his face away from God, as if to say, "Oh no—the Lord's going to remind me of all the terrible things I did." There was a conflict within the heart of Moses.

Another thing he might have been thinking was, *What about my wife and kids? What about my business? Things are looking good; I am comfortable. Besides, I'm eighty years old. Why don't you go get some young buck to do this job?* On the other hand, he may also have been thinking, *Yes, I need to go to Egypt. My brother and sister are still there; my people are suffering. Somebody needs to go deliver them.* It was like he had a devil on one shoulder and an angel on the other.

And this thought may even have come to him: *This is the call of Almighty God! How honored I would be to be used of Him—to finally make a difference with my life, instead of just tending sheep on some mountain.*

This is the conflict that you and I face in America. The bush is burning and God wants us to do something. Every single person who is a true, born-again Christian, anyone who considers himself a disciple of Jesus Christ, has been called to go into all the world and make disciples. Are we too comfortable, or do we want to do something significant?

The same struggle that Moses had is going on in us. Throughout church history we see one truth very clearly: God brings deliverance for others through believers. It's not through a strong military or political unity or more education or better communication with other countries. History says that none of those things work. I believe this burning bush that we face today in America is calling believers to turn to the Lord.

By looking at how God dealt with Moses, we can gain some insight into our own spiritual struggles. In this passage, Moses raises four objections to God, two of which we will cover in this chapter. God's response to Moses shows us how we can answer the call of the burning bush, just as he did.

OBJECTION 1: "WHO AM I?"

Right after God commands Moses to go to Egypt, Moses raises his first objection: "Who am I that I should go to Pharaoh and bring the children of Israel out of Egypt?" (Exod. 3:11). This question, whether asked in humility or in pride, focuses the attention in the wrong place—on Moses. This is a typical human error, even in trying to follow God. It becomes a major obstacle toward truly following God and truly hearing what He's saying through the burning bush. It was Moses' problem, and it's still a problem today. We get sidetracked.

One of the victims of the September 11 attacks was a chaplain of the New York Police Department, dearly beloved by many of the firemen. At his memorial service, many were reminded of a statement he always said: "Do you want to make God laugh? Just tell him your plans for tomorrow." How foolish it is for you and me to think of our plans over and above God's! But that's what we're doing when we say, "Who am I?" God has a plan—in fact, that's what He was saying to Moses at the burning bush: "Moses, I have a plan. I'm calling you to go to Egypt." But Moses responded, "Who am I?"

Look at how God answers Moses: "He said, 'But I will be with you, and this shall be the sign for you, that I have sent you: when you have brought the people out of Egypt, you shall serve God on this mountain.'" (Exod. 3:12). He didn't even answer Moses' question! Moses asked, "Who am I?" and God replied, "That's irrelevant. The point is I will be with you. Who cares who you are? It's as good as done. Just get over there and do it; I guarantee you'll be back here in a few months worshipping Me right here at this mountain."

That's God's answer. And when you and I ask the same kinds of questions of God, He answers, "I will be with you." You don't need any more than that. But this is our struggle: We get sidetracked by the "who am I?" question. The Protestants and Catholics in Northern Ireland, the Muslims and Jews in Jerusalem, those who attacked on September 11 and many cults and false teachers are caught up in the same question. I pray that God will help the church in America to get past the "who am I?" question and finally hear God say, "I will be with you."

When God calls you to do something, He's going to complete it. You were brought to Jesus Christ for a purpose. God has a plan for you, and when He's finished He'll take you home. You won't continue to breathe air for one minute without having a purpose to fulfill. This is a promise from God to every true believer.

Are you bothered by the downward spiral in our culture, the number of abortions, the atrocities, the families falling apart? I'm sure that bothers you and grieves you. We complain about it, we talk about it, we wonder why nothing is done to stop it.

Do you understand that this is the call of God in your life? He is bringing something to your attention. No wonder you're so bothered by this! This is the burning bush experience, and you need to listen up. You are not a Christian for nothing. You have a job to do. You have a calling—don't give Him a busy signal! He's calling every believer in America to be a disciple-maker for Christ. Maybe there's one particular area that really bothers you, really burdens you. Maybe it's kids. Maybe it's the church. Whatever it is, pick it up and say, "Lord, I'll do it."

I heard about a guy in Chicago—a Christian like you and me—who had done quite well for himself. He worked as a stockbroker and drove a really nice car. It bothered him that his nice car was getting abused in the parking lot—big scratches down the side, a light kicked in. Some juvenile delinquents were messing with his stuff. When his place of business got graffiti all over it, he really got ticked off.

Finally it occurred to him that maybe he was supposed to do something about all these kids committing crimes, shooting each other, wrecking his car and ruining his place of business. *Maybe I should help these kids*, he said to himself. This same man happened to love baseball, and he thought, *Maybe I could help organize a baseball league for the inner-city kids in Chicago.*

A few years later, with a huge league and all kinds of teams, he said, "I've learned that if kids play on the same team and hear the gospel when they're nine, ten or eleven, they don't shoot each other when they're fifteen, sixteen or seventeen." Here is a man affecting the lives of hundreds of kids because he dared to really believe God was with him. That's all he is—a believer. He believed and took what was irritating him so much and used it for God.

I heard an amazing story from Olan Hendrix when he came to speak to the elders and staff at my church. Though elderly, Olan has been powerfully used of God in many ways, and he gave our leadership a great deal of help, encouragement and guidance. But his early years were a different story. He grew up in a tough area in one of the southern states.

"My mom died when I was about ten and my father raised me, but that was very difficult because my dad was a drunk," he said. "By the time I was thirteen years old, I felt like something had to change, because I was pretty much living on the street. So I found my father in a bar and got him to sign a paper that said I was seventeen (I was a big kid for thirteen). Then I joined the Navy and fought in World War II—at thirteen years old!"

After two years on a Navy ship, Olan came home and decided to go to college (even though he never went to high school!). With his tuition paid by the GI Bill, he registered at a small college and started looking for a place to live. He found a boardinghouse run by an old lady who let him and two other students live there on one condition: that they let her read the Bible to them at supper. He said, "Hey, no problem, lady. I can deal with that." Little did those students know what effect the Scriptures would have on them!

"All three of us are in full-time ministry today," Olan said. "All three of us were led to Christ by that old lady, who could have easily said, 'Who am I? I am just an old lady.'"

That's just what Moses said: "Who am I? I'm an old man." After all, he was eighty years old! But if you're still breathing, you have a purpose. If you've been saved by Jesus Christ, God has a plan for you. Don't foolishly follow your own plan. Ask the Lord what His plan is, and trust that He will be with you.

OBJECTION 2: "GOD, WHAT IS YOUR NAME?"

After God said, "I will be with you; it's as good as done," Moses came up with another question (isn't he just like us?): "If I come to the people of Israel and say to them, 'The God of your fathers has sent me to you,' and they ask me, 'What is his name?' what shall I say to them?" (Exod. 3:13). Moses was saying, "Lord, I don't know enough." It's interesting how many times Moses uses "I" in Exodus 3 and 4: "Who am I? . . . I don't know this. . . . I can't do that." As one old preacher put it, Moses had an "I" problem!

One point in this passage needs to be clarified: It sounds like Moses didn't know what God's name was. This is puzzling, because he knew God's name was Yahweh. That name was used for God since before Abraham's time. So why would Moses ask for God's name?

Bible scholars call this a Hebrewism. It's a Jewish figure of speech which means about the same as asking, "What is the significance of this?" In other words, Moses is afraid the Israelites are going to respond with the Hebrew equivalent of "What are you talking about? So what?" He's asking God, "How do I answer them? What is the significance of who You are?"

With that in mind, consider the answer God gives: "I AM WHO I AM." And he said, "Say this to the people of Israel, 'I AM has sent me to you.'" (Exod. 3:14). He is saying, "I AM the One who Is." One theologian says it means "I am and will be present." God is saying to Moses, "I am what you need." How's that for significance? Moses has all these questions and God says, "I AM . . ." and lets Moses fill in the blank. "I AM the strength you need; I AM the dedication you need; I AM the money you need; I AM the future you are worried about. I AM all that, Moses. Fill in the blank."

Every one of us has a blank, and we sit before God, asking, "What is the significance of all this?" And He says, "Fill in the blank. I am it." We've been given a blank check and God is saying, "Trust Me and fill it in." He's challenging Moses—and each of us—to be a believer.

This came home very personally to me back when I was in college. I was enrolled full-time, earning money for school and working in youth ministry every free minute I had— helping to run a coffeehouse, working on Christian music festivals, doing beach and street ministry. I was working hard at my job, studying all the time and seeing many lives touched in the ministry—but I had a need. I was lonely. So I said to God, "Lord, it really would be nice if I had a girlfriend and eventually a wife."

The Lord challenged me to fill in that blank. He said, "I am your future spouse. I am your companion. I am the one you need," and I took that seriously. I put God in the blank in my life. And now, after being married for more than twenty-five years, I can tell you that God picked a better wife than I ever could have. I didn't pick her. God did. I didn't know how well she would fit with me and what a great pastor's wife she would be. I didn't know how well everything would work out when I let God fill in the blank.

And that was just the first blank in my life. I have other blanks. So do you. You always will. So did Moses. So God said, "I AM WHO I AM. Fill in the blank with Me." He'll meet your need. He'll take care of you. I don't know what He'll do, but I know He'll provide. There are other blanks in my life which God hasn't supplied, so instead He supplied Himself. I challenge you today to be a believer and let God fill in the blank.

Chapter 7

Don't Give Up

The Lord still speaks today, though maybe not through burning bushes. He speaks through people, through the Word of God, through preachers, through circumstances, crises and difficulties. God speaks to human hearts. In fact, I don't think anyone would ever come to church if God didn't somehow move them, nudge them, cajole them, ask them, convince them, convict them. That's God at work.

The problem is that when God speaks, not everyone hears Him—and I don't mean that God doesn't speak loudly enough! When God spoke to Moses through the burning bush, Moses could hear it just fine. The problem wasn't external. The problem was inside Moses—in his heart, in his mind. It's the same today. God is still speaking to human hearts. He still speaks to people. The question is, do we hear him? Do we listen?

Moses heard God tell him, "I want you to deliver My people, who are enslaved in Egypt. I hear their cries and I am calling on you, Moses. Go do it" (see Exod. 3: 10). God had also answered two of Moses' objections to the plan. But instead of listening to God, Moses was thinking about his life situation. He had been a very handsome, educated, successful young man, but now, several years later, he was beaten down.

Have you noticed how life on this sinful planet has a way of beating us down? Whether it's unmet goals, unfulfilled dreams, illnesses, difficulties, trials, questions or promises broken, we get beaten down, and that's the voice Moses was hearing. God was speaking, but Moses was hearing that lesson of life he had heard so many times before—that life will let you down, that things don't work out the way you hoped. "You know, that's life. That's just the way it is." Don't you hear it?

We are all in the same dilemma. We can hear the words of the Lord, but our life lessons are screaming at us. We've been beaten down. Life has taught us some tough lessons. The pain and hurt scream so loudly, we can't really hear God's words. What do we do? Just what God does with Moses: Identify the root cause and deal with it. God identifies two root causes in the objections of Moses in chapter 4 of Exodus.

OBJECTION 3:
"WHAT IF THEY DON'T BELIEVE ME?"

In the previous chapter of Exodus, God had answered two of Moses' objections to going to Egypt, but he still had more: "What if they do not believe me or listen to me and say, 'The Lord did not appear to you'?" (4:1, NIV). Moses was ready to give up before he even got started! In just the same way, many people don't even become believers because they give up before they even give it a chance. We all tend to give up when we focus on the "what-ifs" instead of on God's work.

The "what-ifs" is a disease—an epidemic that infiltrates churches and gives pastors serious problems. It leads denominations to lose their focus and calling from God. It brings marriage difficulties and discourages believers from joining in the work of the church. It destroys what God wants to do and silences His words. It was screaming so loudly to Moses that he couldn't even hear what God was saying. Imagine this guy telling God Almighty, "What if, Lord?"—as if God hadn't thought about that! But are we any different?

Sometimes, of course, you have to ask, "What if?" It wouldn't be wise to ignore possible pitfalls in your church or in your life. God is not bothered by that at all. But being prudent and wise is not what this passage is about. Moses is trying to make a major life decision based on "what if?"! God doesn't mind you asking, "What if?"; He just minds you living on the basis of "what if." And that is where Moses was.

How do you cure the "what-ifs"? Let's see how God cures Moses':

> The Lord said to him, "What is that in your hand?" He said, "A staff." And he said, "Throw it on the ground." So he threw it on the ground, and it became a serpent, and Moses ran from it.
>
> But the Lord said to Moses, "Put out your hand and catch it by the tail"—so he put out his hand and caught it, and it became a staff in his hand—"that they may believe that the Lord, the God of their fathers, the God of Abraham, the God of Isaac, and the God of Jacob, has appeared to you."
>
> Again, the Lord said to him, "Put your hand inside your cloak." And he put his hand inside his cloak, and when he took it out, behold, his hand was leprous like snow.
>
> Then God said, "Put your hand back inside your cloak." So he put his hand back inside his cloak, and when he took it out, behold, it was restored like the rest of his flesh. "If they will not believe you," God said, "or listen to the first sign, they may believe the latter sign. If they will not believe even these two signs or listen to your voice, you shall take some water from the Nile and pour it on the dry ground, and the water that you shall take from the Nile will become blood on the dry ground." (Exod. 4:2–9)

When Moses said, "What if?" he was questioning the very word of God that came to him. God's answer was, "Look at my works." God gave him three miracles to perform, and said, "Use these works to prove yourself and God's work." In other words, God said, "Instead of focusing on the 'what-ifs,' focus on My work." That's precisely what you and I need to do when we are focused on the "what-ifs." We need to turn our attention to what God is doing.

I'm sure you are tempted to say, "It would be nice if God gave me three miracles I could whip out; Moses had it easy." But the New Testament declares that you and I have more power, more ability, more energy from God given to us than anybody in the Old Testament. We have the Holy Spirit—God within us—which is why we don't have to have Him speak audibly to us as Moses did. We can hear Him in our consciences; He can speak to us and convict us of sin. We can focus on the "what-ifs," or we can focus on God's work in us by the Holy Spirit. That's true for any New Testament believer.

When we started a church in the fall of 1980, I really had the "what-ifs." What if nobody comes? What if the "wrong" people come—people whose lives are really messed up—and they are so uncomfortable to be around that no one else wants to come? What if they don't give enough money to keep the church going? What if we never get a building? If you started asking all the "what-ifs," you'd close your doors and give up. But in that early stage the Lord said to me, "Don't look at 'what-ifs'; look at what I can do—what I have done for others and what I have done in the Scriptures. Look at my works."

I think one reason we have a problem with "what-ifs" is because we don't know the Word of God. Have you looked at what God has done before? Have you talked with other believers and heard what God has done in their lives? Have you used these to build your faith and get away from the "what-ifs"? If not, the "what-ifs" will dominate you.

I remember I had the "what-ifs" when we were trying to build our first building. We had all the difficulties you can imagine. On the day that the slab was poured, we had cement trucks coming and a lot of volunteer help. If it had rained, it would have blown everything. And it was raining all over that day—except on our property! The cement trucks were literally arriving with their windshield wipers on. See what God can do?

We had a huge "what-if" once we got into the building: What if we can't pay the mortgage? We knew that if we didn't double the church's income within three months, we were out of business. What happened? We doubled attendance in three months! We were the fastest-growing church in the state of New Jersey in 1986, according to statistics I read years later. We grew by 220 percent. It is incredible what God can do when a group of people sacrifice and give of their time and energy. They wouldn't believe the "what-ifs"; they believed God. That is what it is going to take for you too to get over the "what-ifs."

Have you noticed what Moses' "what-ifs" were based on? "What if they do not believe me or listen to me and say, 'The LORD did not appear to you'?" (Exod. 4:1, NIV). "What-ifs" are often based on you—how you're going to look and what people are going to think of you. Moses had to get over that. How? He looked at God's work instead of at himself.

I think our country is lost in the "what-ifs." It's certainly true of the media; commentators and news announcers are constantly asking, "What if?" What if the terrorists strike again? What if the economy goes down and we lose our retirement plans? What if we start a war that turns into World War III?

I warn you, believer: Don't be sucked into the "what-if" game. It's just journalism; the media has to have something to talk about. We hear the words of the Lord. For the Christian, the big question is, "What if we don't listen to God?"

Have you ever been so focused on something—a video game, a TV show or a book—that you lost track of everything else? That's what the Lord was trying to get Moses to do—be so focused on God and His work that he would lose his attention on himself. But I'm afraid many of us get so focused on the "what-ifs" that when God speaks, we don't even hear Him.

If you have never heard God speaking to you, maybe this is why. You're so focused on "What if they don't believe me?" or "What if they don't listen to me?" or "What if they say, 'You didn't hear the Lord'?" You need to cry out to God, "Oh Lord, deliver me from myself; help me see the work of God." He'll hear you. Look how patient he was with Moses!

OBJECTION 4: "I'M NOT ELOQUENT"

As if three objections were not enough, Moses comes up with another one: "Moses said to the LORD, 'O Lord, I have never been eloquent, neither in the past nor since you have spoken to your servant. I am slow of speech and tongue'" (Exod. 4:10, NIV). The "never-beens" is another spiritual disorder. It focuses on your inabilities, weaknesses, inadequacies and other problems—maybe even problems in other people.

It's a malady that lends itself to sarcastic phrases such as "Oh, that will never work." I can imagine Moses looking at God and saying, "Oh yeah, right! I wasn't born yesterday." He was questioning God; boy, was he gutsy! At least he debated with God, which is more than many of us do. We don't even hear the words of the Lord clearly enough to debate Him! We are too focused on ourselves.

Moses heard the word, but asked questions. And this "never-been" thing was really in his way. "Lord, it's never been like this. I've never been able to speak well. You know that." How does the Lord answer his "never-beens"? He says, "Who has made man's mouth? Who makes him mute, or deaf, or seeing, or blind? Is it not I, the Lord? Now therefore go, and I will be with your mouth and teach you what you shall speak" (Exod. 4:11–12).

Even Moses' hardened, skeptical attitude is answered by God. And again, God says, "Focus on My work. I'm the one who made your mouth. I'm the one who makes someone blind or makes someone see. I'm the one who puts it together." If you have had a tragedy in your life, such as a physical defect, God planned it. If you are a man, God planned that you be a man. If you are a woman, God planned that you be a woman. If you are five-feet-two-inches or six-feet-five-inches tall, God planned for you to be that height. If you don't think God has planned these things, then you must believe in blind chance.

That was God's answer to Moses: "Moses, look who you're talking to here. I am the Creator; I made your mouth. You wouldn't even be able to talk if it weren't for Me. And now you're telling Me you can't talk? I'm going to use you, Moses. Focus on My work."

How desperately we need to hear those same words! We need to be reminded almost daily that everything is the Lord's. The Lord gave us life, and all we possess is His. We are called by Him to use what He's given us, so we had better get to it and trust that He has a plan. That's what He said to Moses.

Moses still didn't buy it, because he said, "Oh, my Lord, please send someone else" (Exod. 4:13). It's amazing how we can argue with God, isn't it? But at this point Moses had stepped over the line. Notice God's response:

> Then the anger of the Lord was kindled against Moses and he said, "Is there not Aaron, your brother, the Levite? I know that he can speak well. Behold, he is coming out to meet you, and when he sees you, he will be glad in his heart. You shall speak to him and put the words in his mouth, and I will be with your mouth and with his mouth and

will teach you both what to do. He shall speak for you to the people, and he shall be your mouth, and you shall be as God to him. And take in your hand this staff, with which you shall do the signs." (Exod. 4:14–17)

When I started talking about the problem of "never-beens" with the elders in my church, we began calling them "NBs" and we put a different twist on them. Instead of using NBs in a negative way ("Well, that's never happened before; we've never been able to do that") we did it in a positive way. We looked at past obstacles we've overcome and victories we've obtained, and we marked them down as NBs. Not too long ago, I sent a letter to the whole church and told about some of our NBs: never been this many people baptized, never been that many people come to Christ, never been this many people in church. We've had all kinds of "never-beens"!

What we're trying to do by that is focus on what God is doing, on God's work. It's a good idea—and not just for a church, either. Have you ever done this in your own life? Unless you do, I think you'll have the same awful tendency that Moses had (because we are human just like him) to focus negatively on the "never-beens."

This is where journaling comes in handy. Try writing down a few things, whether every day or just once a week, and then look back over it after a period of time. You'll be amazed to see what God has done. It will encourage your faith. It will help you focus on what God is doing in your life. You'll be able to say, "Here are some NBs: I've never done this before and I was able to do it. I've never been able to deal with this, but I did and I accomplished it."

When the World Trade Center came down and the Pentagon was burning on TV, God's words seemed to come upon me, saying very clearly to me just what our government was saying: "It's time to go on the offense now. We can't just play defense." God seemed to be saying, "Sitting around licking your wounds or sitting in church singing praise songs—that's all nice, but I've given you weapons. Go out and use them."

One weapon we have been given as Christians is love: "By this all people will know that you are my disciples, if you have love for one another" (John 13:35). Do the people around you know that you love them and that God loves them too—the people you live with, the people in your neighborhood? It's one of the most powerful weapons we have. Have you used that weapon? We're supposed to be in a spiritual battle, and we're supposed to be taking an offensive position.

Another weapon we have is information—information about God. Do you understand the information about God? Do you know what God has said? Can you use that information? It is a weapon, yet many Christians don't even know how to use it.

Your money is also a weapon. How you invest it, spend it, earn it and use it is a powerful tool. One of the first things our government did to fight terrorism was to track down where the terrorists were getting their money. That's right—they have no power without the financing. Neither does the kingdom of God. God chose to make it that way. He wants us to use our money that way. It's a weapon we have. We can use it or we can waste it.

Prayer is a weapon—a powerful weapon. Do you pray for people who don't know the Lord? Have you ever prayed for the people in the area of your church, and said, "Lord, show us how to reach these people"? Have you prayed, "May they know that we love them and that God loves them too; may they be able to understand the gospel"?

I was telling my elders about what I believed God was saying to us and one of them, a war veteran, said, "That's what Jesus meant when he said, 'Leave the dead to bury their own dead'" (Matt. 8:22). What Jesus was saying was, "You have a job to do; get to it." At that moment I understood that verse like I never understood it before. Jesus is blowing the trumpet; it's time to move out and take the hill.

Chapter 8

You Need to Get Prepared

What do you do after God speaks to you? Now that Moses has had this dramatic encounter with God, what does he do with it?

How come when some people hear God speak, it produces a great difference in their lives—in their attitudes, relationships and values—but when other people seem to have God speak to them, there is little difference?

The answer to that question lies in whether they have let God prepare them or not. God speaks to us, but then He also brings us through a time of preparation, of testing. That's what we see next in the life of Moses.

Imagine being Moses on the side of the mountain with a flock of sheep, just after the bush stops burning, and God stops speaking. Your heart is still thumping in your chest; you can still hear the words of God ringing in your ears. Now you start walking down the mountain in a daze, and things start to rattle around in your head. You're thinking, *I've got to tell my wife; I've got to tell the boss—my father-in-law.*

Think about that. What must that have been like? What do you do after an experience like that? What do you do after God speaks to your heart?

The experience Moses went through is really not much different from the experiences you and I have as Christians.

On the day you were born again, the day you trusted Christ as your Savior, didn't you find yourself saying, "What do I do now?" You had this experience, maybe in a service or in a conversation with a friend, where God spoke to your heart and called you to Himself. What do you do after that?

The big key is preparation. God's going to prepare you now to accomplish something through your life, which is why He called you to Himself. That's what happened in Moses' life, and it's really the same with us. What amazes me as I look at this passage is knowing what lay ahead: Ten plagues were going to come upon Egypt, 2 million-plus people were going to be delivered from slavery to the most powerful nation in the world and the most powerful army in the world was going to be defeated, all because one man believed God! Is that phenomenal or what? At that point in history, there was only one guy—and that was all God needed.

Imagine what God could do through you. Maybe He's given you a passion for a particular group of people or a certain ministry; don't dismiss that. After all, if you had met Moses after he came down from that mountain and he told you, "I'm going to deliver all of Israel from Egypt," you would have laughed in his face. Some dumb sheep farmer is going to take on the most powerful nation in the world? Ridiculous!

But Moses believed what God told him and was ready to obey what God said. When God speaks to you, don't be afraid. It might sound like some fanciful dream, but if God said it, it's going to happen. It's amazing how much God can do through even one person if he will believe Him.

But as I said, the next step for Moses was a period of preparation. God had more things to do in Moses' life, and it all began when he headed out and ran into trouble. Maybe that's happened to you before. You had a dream of something great that God could do through you, but when you headed out to do it, it didn't work out like you thought it would.

I have heard this from a lot of new believers: They become Christians, but a few months or a few years later they say, "It just didn't seem to work out like they said it would." Well, take comfort; you are just like Moses—one of the greatest leaders in all of human history. It didn't work out like he thought either. In fact, it was downright confusing to Moses, because God was testing him.

Just because things don't work out like you think they might doesn't mean God's not at work. He is preparing you, just as he prepared Moses. If He did it with the great leader Moses, of course He will do it with you and me. God has a will and a plan for your life, but to find out what that plan is and to fulfill it—the greatest fulfillment you could possibly have—you have to be prepared by God. Let's look at what we can learn from Moses that will save us a lot of grief and help us get prepared.

When the bush stopped burning, Moses had some time to think about all the things God said to him on his long walk home with the sheep. He concluded that the first person he needed to talk to was his boss and father-in-law, Jethro. So he walked into Jethro's ranch house and said, "Dad, listen. I have to go back to Egypt and see if any of my relatives are still alive. I know it's going to be hard to replace me, but I just have to go back."

He didn't tell Jethro about the burning bush or anything; he just said, "I feel God has told me to do it." Jethro must have sensed his determination, because he replied, "Moses, if God told you to do that, you better do it. Take your wife and your boys and go—with my blessing" (see Exod. 4:18).

So Moses went home and told Zipporah, and they started loading all their belongings on donkeys. They packed up their two sons, both of whom were probably under five years of age, and they headed out for Egypt. Is that a faith-filled risk or what? He just took off—totally dependent on what God told him through the burning bush. And it's just like God that when you start trusting Him for one thing, He shows you more. On the road, He told Moses, "You know, it's going to be tougher than I told you at the bush. Pharaoh has a very hard heart—but I'm going to harden his heart even more. He will oppose you, even if you show him all the miracles I gave you to do."

Moses was probably thinking, *What have I gotten into? Things are going to get rough.* And while he was thinking this through, God added, "Since Pharaoh's heart is so hard, I'm going to kill his firstborn son. That will finally break his heart, so that he lets the people go" (see Exod. 4:21–23).

By this time, evening was coming on, so they set up camp for the night. And this is where the story gets weird—there is no other word to describe it. Exodus 4:24 says that "tthe Lord met him and sought to put him to death." Many theologians suggest that perhaps Moses got very sick, maybe even suffered a heart attack. We don't know exactly what happened, but it appeared that he was dying. Imagine that—you're just trying to obey God, going where He told you to go, and now you are going to die! So he cried out to God, "Lord, what are you doing? You are trying to kill me, and all I've done is obey you."

Suddenly the guilt came upon Zipporah like a torrential downpour. She knew why this was happening—it was her fault. She took Moses' flint knife, took the diaper off little baby Eleazar, cut off his foreskin and threw it at Moses' feet. "Surely you are a bridegroom of blood to me" (see Exod.4:24–26), she cried, with tears coming down her face.

God had instructed Abraham generations earlier to circumcise every Jewish male within eight days of his birth, as a mark of God's ownership. Zipporah had not obeyed this command. Maybe she felt it was cruel or unnecessary and talked Moses out of it. I don't know. But it was wrong, and she knew it.

And as soon as that foreskin hit Moses' foot, he started feeling fine. (I told you it was a weird story!) The point is that Zipporah was acting like God had not created her, or given her this baby, or called the Jews to Himself. In this small way, she was holding back from God, thinking somehow her way was better than God's way. God was preparing Zipporah—and Moses—for the work He had for them by insisting that they get serious about the issue of obedience. Has He ever done something similar with you?

As Zipporah and the baby calmed down and the tears were being wiped away, there was a cry from outside the tent: "Moses, is that you?" Who could it be? Moses whipped open the tent; it was his brother Aaron, whom he hadn't seen for years! As they hugged and kissed each other, with tears streaming down their faces, Moses must have exclaimed, "What are you doing here?"

"I was in Egypt," Aaron said, "and God came to me. He told me to come out here to meet you."

Moses replied, "Well, I can believe that because you should hear what happened to me." He sat down and told Aaron about the burning bush, about the miracles of the staff turning into a snake and the leprous hand and about Zipporah and the circumcision. They probably stayed up half the night talking and got very little sleep.

The next morning they went to Egypt and called all of the elders of Israel together. When they explained to them all that God had revealed, the elders started to weep and cry out and worship God together, saying, "Thank you, LORD, for hearing us in our distress. We are in deep need, and You have heard our cry" (see Exod. 4:27–31).

It's quite a story—and there are truths in it that you and I need to grab hold of. Many people who decide to follow God enter into a time of confusion. They ask, "What in the world is going on?" But as you can see, way back in the Old Testament,

Moses was trying to follow God and the same thing happened to him. To follow the almighty God doesn't always make sense to our puny little minds. We don't understand the ways of God. But if we follow Him, He will prepare us. That means there will be a time of testing. That's what happened to Moses. And from his story we can see three ways that God prepares us through this testing.

1. LEARNING GOD'S PLAN

The first one is this: We get prepared by learning God's plan. Moses had to learn more clearly what God's plan was, and God gave him a few more details about it. When we become Christians, God begins to teach us about His plan. In fact, that is one of the reasons to attend church. We listen to sermons and get involved in discipleship classes to learn more about God's plan for us. That should be the lifelong quest of anyone who calls himself a Christian. There are two things that Moses learned about God's plan that you and I need to learn as well.

The first is that to truly follow God, you must be willing to leave behind comfort. You have to let comfort take second place in your life. If your number-one quest in life is the American dream, you can't follow God. Jesus said the same thing: "If anyone would come after me, let him deny himself and take up his cross and follow me" (Matt. 16:24).

It's not that the American dream is wrong. You might fulfill the American dream of financial security and peace and all that, but if that's your goal, you are not following God. Your number-one goal needs to be God's plan, not comfort.

Moses was doing really well in Midian—working on a successful sheep ranch with a wife, two little boys and his father-in-law for a boss. Everything was comfortable; why leave? A lot of Christians would have heard God's call and said, "Sorry, Lord, I like it right here." And I guess God would have shopped around for someone else to do His plan. Moses would have missed out on the ten plagues, the parting of the Red Sea and the deliverance of 2 million people. He wouldn't have been able to be used of God—all because he might have said, "I'd rather be comfortable."

So we get a good warning here, don't we? It's not that God doesn't want us to be comfortable; after all, the way He protected and comforted Moses throughout his life was phenomenal. It's just that God doesn't want us to seek comfort first. And I think if Moses were here, he'd say, "Don't let comfort be your god. Follow the Lord, not comfort."

That leads to the second thing Moses learns about God's plan: When you follow God, it's step-by-step, like a staircase. Moses took the first step of faith—"OK, God, I'm going to Egypt"—and God said, "Good. Now here is some other information I need to tell you." Moses obeyed the light that was given to him and God gave him a little more light on his path, and then a little more, and a little more—one step at a time.

We see this pattern throughout the life of Moses. And if a great leader like Moses, who was used to change millions of people's lives, only got it a piece at a time, why do we think that we should get the whole plan at once? We won't. We'll get it a piece at a time, a step at a time.

When I tell people about how my church began, they often respond, "Well, I suppose when you were meeting in your house twenty-one years ago with just a handful of people, you could see a vision of this church with thousands of people and various ministries." No, I couldn't see any of that. I had to take one step at a time.

That's the way God always works with His people. He might show you the big picture, as He did with Moses, but the details will be a long process. God may show you a big dream. Don't forget that dream or give up on it, but realize that how you get there is a step-by-step process. Why does God do it that way? Because more than anything, He wants a relationship with us—a step-by-step, day-by-day interaction and communication. That's what it means to fulfill His plan.

The best guarantee that you will be in God's will tomorrow is to make sure you are in God's will today. Walk with Him now—step-by-step. When he challenges you to take another step, say, "Here I am; send me." When you get there, you won't have all the answers yet, but He will start to reveal them. That's what it means to follow God. It's called walking by faith.

2. TRUSTING GOD'S PLAN

We also get prepared by wholeheartedly trusting God's plan. This is seen in that strange passage in Exodus (4:24–26) where God seems to want to kill Moses because his child was not circumcised. Moses could have forfeited everything and never been able to fulfill God's plan for his life because of neglecting that one little ritual. But God saw it as very serious.

It's just like what God said at the burning bush: "Take your sandals off your feet, for the place on which you are standing is holy ground" (Exod. 3:5). He was saying to Moses, "If you want to follow Me, it's going to take holiness—a wholehearted relationship with Me. You can't hold things back from Me or decide that your way is better than Mine." This translates into our lives the same way. Does it all seem kind of rigid, unnecessary, almost cruel, what God demands?

One word that puts this together and helps make sense of the whole thing is detachment. Let me explain. Suppose you say, "Tomorrow, I'm going to get serious about my diet." So you make a serious effort to stick to it this time. But if, in the freezer, you have three gallons of your favorite ice cream, is that a good idea? Of course not! It would be best if you were detached from that ice cream. You would do a lot better on your diet, right? Or if you decide to quit smoking, but you carry around a pack of cigarettes, is that a good idea? No, because you are going to be tempted to smoke if you have them in your pocket. It would be better if you were detached from those cigarettes, if you are serious about quitting smoking.

When I proposed to my wife, I was saying that I was willing to detach myself, emotionally and physically, from every other female on the planet. The key to intimacy in any relationship is detachment from other relationships. If I am going to be fully attached to her and one with her, I have to be detached from relationships with other women or we cannot have intimacy.

That's what this circumcision issue was all about. God was telling Moses, "If you want to follow Me wholeheartedly, have an intimate relationship with Me and work with Me to deliver your people, you have to be with Me and I have to be with you completely." If God touches on some puny little thing in your life and says, "You shouldn't be doing that," you can't say, "Come on, let's not be so rigid." Remember, that's God speaking to you! Say to Him, "OK, Lord, if that's what you want, wholehearted commitment, you got it." Then God will start showing you more light and using you in more ways.

Don't be afraid to listen to your conscience and to what God is telling you. Detachment is necessary for intimacy and wholehearted commitment. When you decide to follow God, it means you're not going to follow some other things. When you decide to follow God's plan, it means you are going to detach yourself from your plan. If you don't, then you are not following God.

That's precisely what this confusing circumstance in Moses' life was about. Is there something in your life that is confusing you in the same way? God is asking you for everything, for wholehearted commitment. He wants your life. The reason some Christians go on to see God work is because they are willing to take those steps. The reason others don't is because they won't. It's that simple.

3. SHARING GOD'S PLAN

The third way we get prepared is by sharing God's plan. In Exodus 4:28–30, Moses shared what God told him with Aaron; then they shared it with all the elders of Israel. God may reveal His plan to one man to begin with, but He seldom, if ever, works through just one man. Even Jesus called together twelve disciples, who eventually multiplied into churches of hundreds of thousands of people, because God's plan always works through people working together.

This is where a lot of Christians stop—especially American Christians, who think so independently. They think, "Following God's plan for my life is just great, but getting involved with other people leads to conflict, differences of opinion and difficulties." Many churchgoers remain aloof and uninvolved. It's dangerous, because they miss God's plan, God's best for them.

God wants to work through you in a team. "For where two or three are gathered in my name, there am I among them" (Matt. 18:20). He works through people together. God wants to complement your gifts with the gifts of other members of Christ's body, as it says in First Corinthians 12:12–31. If I take my hand and cut it off, my hand is not very useful. But if it stays attached to the body, it can do all kinds of wonderful things. It's the same with you as a part of the Church.

We learn from Moses that if God shows you what He wants you to do, you should attach that to the rest of the body. Share the dream that God has put on your heart with others, and let them join you in accomplishing it. In fact, when God gives a dream and we share it with others, we may discover that God has been talking to them too. It is really exciting how God puts all the pieces together and works it out.

In the book *Halftime*, Bob Buford tells of his struggle with the issue of God's plan for his life and how he learned a similar lesson: "I cannot recall a single thing worth doing that I have accomplished by myself. . . . The individualism so rampant in our culture is an individualism that borders on selfishness." [xi]

Bob goes on to explain how success in business is built on learning to use your gifts and strengths in conjunction with the gifts and strengths of others. Bob began to learn that his strong individualism, which he had seen as a strength, was actually his greatest weakness.

What Bob began to understand was that God was not only giving him a new vision, but was asking him to share what God was calling him to do with other people. It's just what Moses was learning. I think God is calling each one of us as followers to do the same thing: to get involved with other people and to open our lives up to others.

Ron and his wife, Amy, are a young couple in their early thirties. They came to Christ fairly recently, and the dramatic change in their lives has been astounding. As young believers, they have pumped me with questions about the Bible. We have had wonderful times together, learning from the Scriptures. When I first witnessed to Ron a few years ago, his life was really messed up; their marriage was pretty much over, and he was involved with drugs. But now that he has responded to God's call, he has gotten off drugs and he and his wife are back together. It's just wonderful to see God work in his life.

I once asked him what had kept him from coming to Christ, when his wife became a Christian years before. He said, "I kept asking myself, what's it going to cost me? Do I have to go to church every Sunday? Do I have to quit drinking and hanging around with my friends? But now that I've become a Christian, it's worth it—and much more. God gave his only Son, Jesus Christ, for us, paid the penalty for our sins, so that we could be forgiven and enter into a new life. . . . I can't believe how stupid I was."

What keeps a Christian from following God's plan for his life? The same thing—"What's it going to cost me?" I'm pleading with you—take the step; it's worth it. Just as if you were a nonbeliever, take the step. God's not going to hurt you or leave you alone. Don't get caught up in the devilish question "What's it going to cost me?" God will take care of that. It's going to cost you everything, and you're going to give it all and say, "Boy, it was worth everything and more."

Chapter 9

How to Be Delivered by God

Have you ever wondered why the Israelites had to wait through the ten plagues in Egypt before they could be delivered? Why didn't God just deliver them all at once? Why did they have to go through all that rigmarole?

In the same way, I imagine there is one area in your life, one particular sore spot or recurring problem, in which you find yourself asking, "Lord, why don't you just deliver me? Why don't you just change the situation? Why don't you just do it, Lord?"

The answer is found in Exodus 5, when Moses and his brother Aaron went to meet with Pharaoh. I am sure Moses was thinking, *Isn't this fantastic? The Lord is answering our prayers! He's going to deliver us and make us happy!* But God had different ideas. Yes, God delivered them for the purpose of making them happy. But how He delivered them was for the purpose of making them holy. The difference is very crucial.

It is a basic biblical principle: One reason God delivers us and takes us to heaven is for our happiness. There's no doubt about that. I know people who have been delivered from alcohol, drugs, sexual abuse, all kinds of terrible things. God did it because He wanted to make them happy. But how God delivered them—His process of deliverance—was because He wanted to make them holy.

God said that since He is holy, we should be holy (see Lev. 11:45). In other words, God is trying to make us like Himself. And because His deliverance from a problem, a difficult situation or a habit is not just about making us happy, but about making us holy, how He delivers us often differs from what we think He's going to do. That was the confusion we see in Moses in Exodus 5. If you are feeling that same kind of confusion, read on. And don't forget, God's deliverance results in your happiness, but how God delivers you results in your holiness.

When you apply this principle you see the whole story. God may have given you a spouse to make you happy, but how you live out that marriage is all about you becoming holy. God may have delivered you from joblessness and given you a great job for your happiness. But what you go through with your boss and what happens on the job is about your holiness. God is just as concerned about making you holy as happy.

The friends you have are for your happiness, but what happens in those friendships is sometimes not about your happiness at all, but your holiness. God gave you a church to make you happy, but also to make you holy. Maybe some of the conflicts, difficulties or questions you have are about your holiness, not your happiness.

Have you ever looked at your spouse or your church or your job and said, "This is not making me happy"? Should you get a new job, a new spouse, a new church? Maybe that's not the problem at all. You need a new perspective. You need to realize God is doing this to make you holy. That's going to take some work!

Let's look at Exodus 5 and see what principles we can glean about this holiness and happiness thing.

After praying with the elders and getting their blessing, Moses and Aaron went to the palace. Working their way through the different levels of guards, they eventually entered the throne room of Pharaoh, the leader of the most powerful nation in the world. Maybe it was like they show it in a Hollywood movie, with Pharaoh sitting on an elaborate throne in beautiful silk clothing, with a servant on each side waving a big fan—the picture of opulence.

Moses and Aaron, in contrast, had been out in the desert. Moses probably had his shepherd's outfit on. There may have been some perfunctory greetings or introductions—we don't know. But we do know that Moses got right down to business. He looked up at Pharaoh and said, "The Lord God of Israel has spoken. You must let His people go into the desert to hold a festival for the Lord" (see Exod. 5:1). All Moses knew of God's plan at that point was that the Lord had said, "I'll meet you back at this mountain," so he told Pharaoh, "The Lord says, 'Let my people go.'"

Pharaoh must have thought, *Who is this bozo coming in here telling me how to run my country? Who does this guy think he is?* So he said, "Who? I don't know the God of Israel you are talking about. I am god of Egypt. I don't care what this God of yours says; He's not taking my slaves away from their work. Get out of here" (see 5:2).

Moses, being very gutsy at this point, decided to appeal to Pharaoh's business sense. "If we do not go out into the desert and sacrifice to our God, He may strike us down! You could lose your whole workforce. If I were you, I'd let us go" (see 5:3).

But Pharaoh wasn't buying it. "I can see right through you guys. You're not fooling me for a minute. You're just lazy. Now get back to work!" (see 5:4). And he kicked them out of the palace.

To make matters worse, Pharaoh told the slave drivers and foremen, "All this song and dance from Moses and Aaron must mean the slaves have too much time on their hands. So I want just as many bricks made, but I'm not providing straw anymore. [They made bricks by mixing straw with mud.] Go out and scrounge for your own straw" (see Exod. 5:6–11).

Day after day went by, and the Israelites didn't meet their quota of bricks. Finally, the foremen appealed to Pharaoh: "We humble ourselves before you, O great Pharaoh, and we ask you to listen to our plea. Why are you being so harsh to us? We have been working hard. Now you won't give us straw, but we are supposed to make just as many bricks. We can't do it" (see 5:15–16).

Pharaoh responded, "You're just lazy—that's your problem! Otherwise you wouldn't be asking to go out in the desert and worship the Lord. Now get back to work. You'd better produce just as many bricks or you're in big trouble" (see 5:17–18).

As the foremen left the palace, they met Aaron and Moses. They walked up to Moses, pointed a finger at him and said, "You arrogant jerk! May God judge you for what you've done! Now we're a stench to Pharaoh, and he's going to kill us. You and your big ideas about delivering everybody—why don't you just leave us alone?" (see 5:20–21).

Moses, if you remember, had heard something like this years earlier, when one of the Israelites said, "Who made you a prince and a judge over us?" (2:14). What did Moses do back then? He ran away to Midian. Guess what? When that Israelite said, "I hope God judges you," Moses ran again—except this time, he ran to the Lord. What he said to the Lord is a key to what God wants us to learn about His process of deliverance: "O Lord, why have you done evil to this people? Why did you ever send me? For since I came to Pharaoh to speak in your name, he has done evil to this people, and you have not delivered your people at all" (5:22–23).

When we seek the Lord for deliverance, sometimes we get confused. It happened to Moses, so why should we expect anything less? Maybe you are in a time of confusion; you just don't understand what's going on. I believe there are some answers here in this story of Moses.

GOD'S DELIVERANCE REQUIRES COURAGE

The first one is seen at the very beginning of Exodus 5: God's deliverance requires courage. If you think you can follow God without a lot of courage, you are sadly mistaken. Verse 1 says, "Afterward Moses and Aaron went and said to Pharaoh, 'Thus says the Lord, the God of Israel, "Let my people go."'" Notice too that after Pharaoh says no, they make another appeal: "Then they said, 'The God of the Hebrews has met with us. Please let us go a three days' journey into the wilderness that we may sacrifice to the Lord our God, lest he fall upon us with pestilence or with the sword.'" (Exod. 5:3).

Moses was pretty gutsy to do this, because Pharaoh, by all accounts, was not only the most powerful man in the world at that time, but also a raging egomaniac—if he was Rameses II, as many historians say. Consider this inscription on the wall of his mortuary temple: "King of Kings am I, Rameses II. If anyone would know how great I am and where I lie, let him surpass just one of my works." Even in death, he was arrogant and boastful! You have to admit that if Moses was going to be used as a deliverer, he had to be very courageous to stand up to such a man.

It's the same for you and me. To be a deliverer for yourself, your spouse, your children or someone else takes great courage. You will face great opposition, maybe even an egomaniac like Pharaoh; don't expect anything less. In fact, it seems to be part of God's process, not just to make Moses and Israel happier, but to make them holier.

I have a close friend and coworker named Brian Snyder who has demonstrated tremendous courage to me and our entire church. You see, Brian's oldest daughter was diagnosed with leukemia at the age of eighteen. She had fought off leukemia when she was four years old and then, to everyone's shock and horror, it came back.

Many people faced with the potential loss of their children not once but twice would lose courage. But Brian had learned from his own rough childhood, as well as the rough times when his four-year-old daughter was battling leukemia, that if you're ever going to see God's deliverance in your life, you need to have the courage to trust God when things are tough.

So, Brian set out courageously to lead not only himself but his daughter, wife, other children and our church family through the battle for his daughter's life. His statements of belief, hope and determination in the midst of endless trips to the doctors showed great courage. This time, however, Brian's daughter didn't win the battle with leukemia. Brian had to say good-bye to his eighteen-year-old daughter and give her into the hands of God. Grief, tears and sorrow followed. But even in the face of such a great loss, Brian was incredibly strong, mighty and courageous as he led his family, our church and many others through the sorrow to a strong hope in God.

It has been a few years since his daughter's death, and Brian and his family are doing very well. I attribute this fact to Brian's courage. He demonstrated and lived out the truth we all need to learn: God's deliverance in, through, around and past any problems is only found when we have the courage to believe that He is right and loves us totally, no matter what. God is in control all of the time, so we are always right to have courage.

Whether you are Brian Snyder facing the death of your child or Moses facing an egomaniac oppressor, the key to being God's deliverer is courage. Do you have the courage to trust God in the midst of a financial need or a troubled marriage? It may not be what Moses faced in Egypt, but it calls for the same response. Do you have courage? Without courage you can't see deliverance. It is the first step to happiness and holiness in your life.

If Moses was going be God's man and do God's work, he needed to face the opposition and even to lose the first battle. God designed it that way. If you are looking at your life and saying, "I've lost a lot of battles," that's OK. Do you think that's not what God wants? Do you think God's not doing a work in you by losing a battle? He worked in Moses and the Israelites that way. He'll win the war; you'll see.

God will deliver you, just as He delivered Israel, but how God does it sometimes confuses us. We say, "Why don't you just do it?" And He responds, "I have a plan to make you holy." Maybe some failure will help; maybe some disappointment and discouragement. And in the midst of it, if you can be courageous and continue to have hope and believe, God will change you. When I read Moses' prayer at the end of Exodus 5, it gets me thinking that prayer is more about changing me than actually changing the situation and getting God to do what I want. It's God working on me.

GOD'S DELIVERANCE REQUIRES RENEWAL

You might criticize Moses for complaining to God in Exodus 5:22–23, but I compliment him for it. The last time this kind of pressure came on him, he ran away from God in bitterness, confusion and anger. This shows another thing we learn from Moses: God's deliverance requires renewal.

It's easy to walk away from God and hardly even know it. You are just not talking to Him anymore; the relationship just isn't as close as it used to be. It wasn't God who moved—it was you. But this time Moses didn't do that. He went back to God. Even though he was complaining and asking why, he was still trying to communicate with God.

I'm sure, in Moses' mind, he was comparing himself with Pharaoh: *I want to do what is right, but Pharaoh is only thinking about himself. I am concerned for human relationships,*

but Pharaoh is concerned about his reputation. I'm leading people;
I'm not just pushing them around. This tyrant is subjugating people
for his own ends. I know Your will, Lord; all this guy knows is his
own will. So, Lord, here's me; here's him. How come You are not on
my side? It looks like You're on his side. He's winning!

Have you ever prayed like that? It's not all bad to talk
with God that way. The most important thing is that Moses
was still talking to God, renewing and getting deeper in his
relationship with Him. That is what God wanted all along!
God knew what would happen to Moses and how he would
respond. God knew he would try to justify himself and
complain. But at least Moses went to God, and that's what
God wants.

God wants us to be renewed day by day, and I don't know
about you, but I need it daily. Reading Scripture, praying,
reading a good Christian book, talking with other Christians,
going to church—I need renewal daily, weekly, monthly.
Why? Because, like Moses, I often get confused. I would
suggest that if you do not sense a need for daily renewal, it
may be because you are either not trying to follow Him very
closely or He's recently answered some questions for you and
given you that "peace . . . which surpasses all understanding"
(Phil. 4:7).

Someone once said that mystery is not the absence of
meaning, but the presence of more meaning than we can
comprehend. Moses was caught in a mystery. He didn't
understand all that was going on. Mystery will happen in your
life and my life as well—we don't understand; we can't figure
it out; it makes no sense. Our problem is simply that we lack
the IQ to comprehend God and the mysteries by which He
operates.

I have known a number of people with rather high IQs
who display an enviable ability to comprehend things quickly
and give great answers to tough questions. It often seems to

me that such intelligence must be a great asset.

But I've also noticed over the years that the great strength of "being smart" can work against such people. These people, whom I will call intellectuals, can get in a mind-set where they actually rule out mystery. They think they can figure out anything, even (though they would never say it out loud) God. So they struggle to trust Him in mystery when a less intelligent person like myself, who easily sees his intellectual limitations, finds it much easier to just say, "I don't know, but God does."

I decide to trust God and realize I am not within His dimension of thinking. These intellectuals, however, find that a very uncomfortable realization because they have not often dealt with not knowing the answers to tough questions. But walking with God will always involve mystery, no matter how intelligent or enlightened you may be. If one cannot accept mystery, one cannot accept God.

We often do not understand God's methods or the reasons behind them, but we can rest in the knowledge that God is trustworthy. You may be struggling in mystery right now, trying to figure it all out before you decide to trust Him. Moses decided it was safe to trust God before he figured it out, and so God could use Moses as a deliverer. God can use you too, but only if you can trust Him with what you can't figure out.

Mystery is not the absence of meaning; it's the presence of more meaning than we can comprehend. Moses said, "Lord, I have decided to take the courageous step of trusting You." Can you do the same?

Chapter 10

LEARNING TO LISTEN TO GOD

In the last chapter, we left Moses in despair, questioning God. If you have never been in a similar place in your life, I guarantee that someday you will be. What Moses learned, and what you and I need to learn, is how to listen to God. As he finished his discouraged prayer at the end of Exodus 5, Moses was in the place that we all get to sometimes, where he desperately needed to hear from the Lord. He needed to hear God speak into his life—into his burdens, problems and heartaches, and even into his joys, successes and victories. But for God to do that, Moses had to learn how to listen.

Let's look at what God has to say:

But the Lord said to Moses, "Now you shall see what I will do to Pharaoh; for with a strong hand he will send them out, and with a strong hand he will drive them out of his land."

God spoke to Moses and said to him, "I am the Lord. I appeared to Abraham, to Isaac, and to Jacob, as God Almighty, but by my name the Lord I did not make myself known to them. I also established my covenant with them to give them the land of Canaan, the land in which they lived as sojourners. Moreover, I have heard the groaning of the people of Israel whom the Egyptians hold as slaves, and I have remembered my covenant. Say therefore to the people of Israel, 'I am the Lord, and I will bring you out from under the burdens of the Egyptians, and I will deliver you from slavery to them, and I will redeem you with an outstretched arm and with great acts of judgment. I will take you to be my people, and I will be your God, and you shall know that I am the Lord your God, who has brought you out from under the burdens of the Egyptians. I will bring you into the land that I swore to give to Abraham, to Isaac, and to Jacob. I will give it to you for a possession. I am the Lord.'"

Moses spoke thus to the people of Israel, but they did not listen to Moses, because of their broken spirit and harsh slavery. (Exod. 6:1–9)

I believe these nine verses are a universal passage. In other words, they are generic; they will work for everyone. What we see here is a great example of how people in desperate times need to hear God speak. God has things to say to us, but we can hear Him only if we are listening. Whether we hear Him or not depends on us, not Him.

We often act like God hasn't spoken when He has—very clearly—but we are like the Israelites, who were so discouraged they couldn't even hear God. God spoke; they just couldn't hear it. It is crucial that we learn to turn our minds and hearts to be able to hear God speak.

Moses was pretty discouraged too. He had gotten to the point where he was saying, "Lord, why did You send me here? You haven't rescued the people at all!" It's like he was dialing 911. He was saying, "Lord, You have to answer my questions, and You have to answer them now." Have you ever been there? You have to get that desperate to really hear God. You have to get to the place where you throw away all formalities and pray in emergency mode.

And, of course, God answers. God speaks when we cry out to Him in need, just as He spoke to Moses. Moses' questions had piled up; he had problems; he didn't understand what was going on. He had a difficult situation with Pharaoh, and now the Israelites were rejecting him again. I am sure he also had pressures at home with his wife and kids that are not even spoken of in this passage.

Sometimes we're a lot like Moses. We get saved and start following the Lord, but then this doesn't happen like you thought it would, and that doesn't happen like you thought it would, and this doesn't change, and that doesn't change. The next thing you know, questions start piling up, pushing down on you until you get to the point where you cry out, "Lord, I need answers—and I need them now!"

God will speak—but you have to be listening. I guarantee you God is speaking; this is revealed over and over throughout the Scriptures. The question is not whether God is speaking, but whether you are hearing. This passage tells us how we can learn how to hear God speak. We can see the answers in how God spoke to Moses and what He said.

"I AM"

Sometimes God's answer is, "I am." Notice that several times God said to Moses, "I am the LORD." This repetition of "I am" is God's answer. Notice also that "I am" is not really an answer to Moses' questions! "Lord, You haven't done anything to rescue the people yet. Why did You bring me here?" In all nine verses of this passage, there's no answer to Moses' questions—at least, not directly. This is not uncommon for God. God often speaks to us in indirect ways.

Is God just being elusive, or tricky or aloof? Why doesn't He just give me an answer? Here's why: God is holy, just and truthful, and often we aren't. Often our minds are so twisted, our thoughts so bent by sin and the sinful environment we live in, that we can't think in pure, just, truthful terms. When God gives us an answer, we don't even hear it. We can't understand it.

Remember God's answer? "I am the LORD," repeated over and over again. Why would God repeat something, if not for emphasis? This is the key thing Moses needed to remember. Why did the message He told Moses to give to Israel begin and end with "I am the LORD"? Because they needed to understand that He is the LORD!

What does it mean when God says, "I am the LORD"? First of all it means, "Moses, you are not the LORD." Second, it means, "Moses, neither Pharaoh nor anyone else in the world is the LORD, either." And last, it means, "Hello, Moses! This is the Lord speaking. Your 911 call got through!"

What could be more comforting for anyone in desperate straits to hear than "I am the LORD"? I don't know if you've ever been in the kind of desperate situation Moses was in, but I have—or at least it felt that desperate. I felt crushed, and I cried out to God for answers. No one else could comfort me. Anything anyone said seemed so trite, so artificial. When it comes to some questions in your heart and mind, or some obstacles you need to get over, there is no friend or pastor or counselor who can help you. You need to hear from the Lord. He's the only one who can fix it.

In the old days when I was a kid, we carried our baseball mitts around all the time and were always having games. It wasn't as formalized as it is today, with leagues and all that stuff. We just found an empty lot, picked teams and started playing. Almost always the first person picked was my older brother Don, because then you were practically guaranteed to win. He could hit the ball farther, run faster, catch anything. That's the guy you wanted on your team.

When I hear God say to Moses, "I am the LORD," I hear Him saying, "Hey, I am on your team—you can't lose! Why are you sitting here crying like a loser and complaining like the game is already over? Maybe things don't look too good here in the first inning, but we're going to win. I guarantee it."

And when the Lord speaks to you and me, He often doesn't tell us all the details. He doesn't need to. All He needs to tell us is "I am the LORD." If you are on His team, you win. At the end of the Bible it says that those who are loyal and faithful, who follow Christ with all their hearts, go to heaven and have a wonderful eternity with Him forever. You win!

We often get so negative about our churches, our families, our personal lives, our jobs. We sound like a bunch of losers when the truth is that we are winners! The Lord is on our team. We can't lose, no matter what happens. Paul the apostle put it this way: "For if we live, we live to the Lord, and if we die, we die to the Lord. So then, whether we live or whether we die, we are the Lord's" (Rom. 14:8). In other words, he says, we can't lose. We need that perspective.

"I WILL"

A second thing we learn here about listening to God is that sometimes His answer is "I will." Notice the repetition of "I will" in Exodus 6:6–8—seven times! "I will bring you out from under the burdens of the Egyptians . . . I will deliver you from slavery to them, and I will redeem you . . . I will take you to be my people, and I will be your God . . . I will bring you into the land . . . I will give it to you for a possession." Why would God repeat something over and over again? For emphasis—to make sure we get the point: "I am the Lord and I will do what I promised."

Notice also that God put it in very broad terms; this is big-picture stuff. He told Moses about the new land they would live in and about being delivered from slavery to the Egyptians. He didn't say anything about the ten plagues, crossing the Red Sea, the Ten Commandments or the numerous battles they would fight to win the Promised Land. God spoke in big-picture terms, in long-range plans. If you and I are going to hear God speak, we have to see life as God sees it: in big-picture terms and long-range plans.

Here's another thing about God's "I will" that you don't see in the English translation. In the original Hebrew, the words I will are not written in future tense, but in what is called "prophetic perfect tense," which is past tense. In other words, God is talking about something that is going to happen in the future as if it has already happened!

The promises of God are so certain to happen that God speaks about them as if they have already taken place—and from God's point of view, they already have. He's in eternity; He doesn't see a past, present and future. It's already done. So when He says, "I will," it's as good as done! It's in the bag. It's over.

This reminds me of a passage from Isaiah 55:

> For my thoughts are not your thoughts,
>   neither are your ways my ways, declares the LORD.
> For as the heavens are higher than the earth,
>   so are my ways higher than your ways
>   and my thoughts than your thoughts.
> "For as the rain and the snow come down from heaven
>   and do not return there but water the earth,
> making it bring forth and sprout,
>   giving seed to the sower and bread to the eater,
> so shall my word be that goes out from my mouth;
>   it shall not return to me empty,
> but it shall accomplish that which I purpose,
>   and shall succeed in the thing for which I sent it. (55:8–11)

So when God says, "I will," you can count on it. It's going to happen. For many of us, however, the trouble we have with listening to God is that we don't know what God said He will do.

Do you know the Scriptures? Do you know the promises

of God? He has already spoken. He has already said what He will do; Moses was simply being reminded by God of what He had already said.

I read a story about an old Scottish woman who worked long hours every week taking in laundry and tucking the money away to send her son to college. Finally the day came when her son could go to college. This lady was a strong Christian, and she often told her son that God had blessed her with this job and with the ability to wash clothes so he could be the first person in their family to go to college.

When he came back from college over the summer, he was a little irritated by his mother's constant talk about God—how He had provided for her personally, how He had saved her soul and was going to take her to heaven. In his mind, it didn't jive with what he had learned at college about the vastness of the universe and how insignificant humans are.

Finally, about halfway through the summer, he became so frustrated that, as kind and as nice as his mother had been to him, he felt obligated to try to help her get the perspective he had learned at college.

"Mom," he said, "the way you talk about all that God provides and how God cares is just not realistic. Don't you understand how little and insignificant you are compared to the universe? Why would God lose anything if He lost you? If God didn't take you to heaven, what would He really lose? What would you really lose? You are just one of a multitude of people who have been born on this planet throughout human history, and the earth itself is just a speck in the vastness of space. Your idea that God answers your prayers is all out of proportion to reality."

His mother must have been taken aback! What do you say to such an argument? So she didn't say anything, and there was a tenseness in the air. She set the table for dinner, they sat down to eat and she prayed for the meal. Then she looked at her son across the table and said, "I have been thinking about what you said. I think in a sense you are right. If the Lord didn't save me, if it wasn't really true that He was answering my prayers and these things just kind of happened, you are right—I wouldn't lose much. But you are wrong about God. If God doesn't answer my prayers, He loses a lot more than I do. God loses His reputation and His character! I am not going to lose much if He's wrong, but He loses everything if He's wrong."

There was a lady who understood what it meant to count on God's Word when He says, "I will"! She was helping her son see the truthful perspective: that God loses everything if His word isn't true. That is precisely what the Lord is saying to Moses: "Don't you understand? If this doesn't happen I lose everything! You might lose a battle or get in trouble, Moses, but in the light of human history, what's the big deal? But for Me it is a big deal, because I said I am going to deliver you from the Egyptians, and I will."

If you are going to listen to God you need to believe that He will do what He says He will do. God's character, His whole person, is based upon that. He will come through for you.

SOME PEOPLE DON'T LISTEN

The third thing we learn from this passage is in Exodus 6:9: "Moses spoke thus to the people of Israel, but they did not listen to Moses, because of their broken spirit and harsh slavery." Sometimes we don't listen to God's answer. It's true— you can be so discouraged you just can't hear God speak. I don't know about you, but I've certainly been there before. It's usually accompanied by criticism, complaining and comparing yourself with other people. Things aren't going right and you get discouraged, just like the Israelites.

It's easy for us to point a finger at the Israelites and say, "What a shame—they didn't listen to God!" But we can get to the same place; God speaks and we can't even hear Him. How can we keep that from happening to us? How can we keep ourselves from getting so discouraged that we can't hear God speak?

The answer is found in doing what God told us to do right here in this passage: Recognize who He is ("I am the LORD"), obey and trust what He says ("I will") and thank Him for what we are going to see happen, because it's as good as done.

Wait a minute—what about the reality of a terrible situation? Isn't thankfulness kind of naïve? In response, I'd like to pose a different question: Has an attitude of bitterness ever healed a disabled child, filled a bank account or repaired a leaky toilet? Being thankful doesn't fix the broken lives or bitter losses, but it does transform our spirits as we face them.

Thankfulness is power to your soul. God offers it to us to drive out the spiritually degenerative illness of bitterness and negative thinking. I like to think of thankfulness as God's spiritual air freshener. It replaces the stale odor of resentment with clean, fresh air for the soul to breathe.

For many of us, it's easy to slide into negative thinking, critical words and wanting what we don't have, instead of seeing the truths that God told Moses: "I am the LORD" and "I will do what I promised." The Israelites didn't listen, but we know Moses did, because he went out to fulfill what God called him to do.

If we are having trouble listening to God, perhaps the first step is to confess that we have not been thankful for all God has given, and ask His forgiveness. Then we can ask Him to change our attitudes and give us ears to hear.

Chapter 11

TRUE FREEDOM – GOD'S FREEDOM

Moses, encouraged by God's word to him, went on to confront Pharaoh and was used by God to set the Israelites free. God used ten plagues to free the Israelites from Egypt's bondage (Exod. 7–12). There are a number of principles we can learn from these plagues, especially the last one. For that reason, I'm going to discuss the last plague in the next chapter.

The story of the plagues in Egypt is one of the most significant portions of the Bible, but in order to understand the story, we need to begin with this basic truth: God values freedom. He values it so much that He set the children of Israel free. He sent His Son to earth to die on the cross to set us free from the bondage of our sin. And through all this, God is trying to bring us into the freedom He enjoys Himself.

Have you ever considered the fact that God Almighty is the only one who is truly free? All the planets and stars, all the vegetation, animals and the people on the earth, all the atoms and molecules, are interdependent. But one Person is not dependent upon any of it. God is dependent upon nothing. He's totally independent and free.

While many people think they are free to do whatever they want, we all have to live with physical limitations. We are limited by things such as sight, hearing, endurance, etc. But

God is not limited by a body. He can hear everything. He can see everything. He's free. God is the only one who is free.

That's why one of God's core values is freedom. It's part of His nature. He's the only one who is absolutely free—not dependent, not relying on anything or anyone, not limited by time or space. However, you and I are not free, and we know that. We're limited by our bodies, by our knowledge, by time, by space and in many, many other ways. So freedom to us has always looked very attractive, especially since, as Genesis says, we are created in the image of God (see 1:27). We long for freedom.

How, then, can a human being, in a universe where everything depends on everything else, be free? That's what this story of the ten plagues is all about. It explains how to experience the freedom that only God can bring. In the first nine plagues, two basic principles stand out about how we can get free.

THE NINE PLAGUES

The first plague was upon the Nile River, turning its water into blood (see Exod. 7:14–24). In the Cecil B. DeMille film *The Ten Commandments*, Moses told Aaron to stretch out his staff against the waters, and the water began turning red, radiating out from where he touched the river. That's how Hollywood saw it, anyway.

But the Bible doesn't really say that it was instantaneous like that. Some commentators speculate that a flood from Uganda went through the Sudan swamps, picking up algae and dirt, turning the water red. I don't know whether to buy that or not. Whether God did it naturally or actually turned the water into blood doesn't really matter, because it all happened when Moses said it would, so it's still a miracle called down by God.

But Pharaoh's heart was still hardened and he wouldn't let Israel go. So God brought a second plague on Egypt—a plague of frogs. (Some commentators say the frogs were just trying to get out of the Nile and find some clean water.) The Scriptures tell us that people found frogs in their ovens, in their kneading troughs and in their beds. They were in every Egyptian home—even in the palace! Have you ever been around a swamp at night when the frogs start croaking? It can get pretty loud! I'm sure all the hopping and croaking was driving the Egyptians nuts.

Pharaoh called in Moses and said, "Get rid of these frogs and I'll let your people go. I promise." So Moses prayed and all the frogs died; they piled them up in heaps and they began to stink. But Pharaoh again changed his mind and would not let the people go (see Exod. 8:1–15).

So God told Moses that a plague of gnats would come upon the Egyptians. Some historians say these were mosquitoes, brought on by the flood. I know mosquitoes, because I grew up in Minnesota. They're huge and they're all over the place. We used to go camping in northern Minnesota and up into Canada, and when we closed the screen on the tent at night, we literally couldn't see through the net because of the mosquitoes. And the buzzing would drive us crazy. So I can understand how this could get Pharaoh's attention.

By this time, even some of Pharaoh's officers started believing Moses. In fact, some of his officers said, "Hey, this is the finger of God, Pharaoh; you'd better pay attention." But his heart was hardened again, and he refused to let them go (see Exod. 8:16–19).

God told Moses to come before Pharaoh again and warn him about a plague of flies. It is interesting that this fourth plague, as well as the rest of them, occurred in Egypt but not in Goshen, where all the Israelites lived. God started making a distinction between the Egyptians and the Israelites from then on.

One historian speculates from his research that this insect was *stomoxys calcitrans*, the biological name for a kind of fly that lays 600-800 eggs at a time and multiplies extremely fast. This fly bites the lower extremities of animals and humans and is a major carrier of anthrax. So this plague may have been more than merely annoying; it may have been deadly. Pharaoh called Moses back and said, "Pray that the flies would be removed and I will let you go." Moses prayed, and the flies were gone. And Pharaoh broke his promise again (see Exod. 8:20–32).

So God brought a fifth plague upon Egypt, this time against their livestock. The hand of God struck all of the Egyptian cattle. Pharaoh had his men check on the Israelites' cattle, but they found that none of them had died. It is interesting that God struck the cattle, because the Egyptians worshipped images made to look like bulls. They also worshipped a frog god and a god of the Nile River. Isn't it interesting that God struck the very things they worshipped? But again, Pharaoh's heart was hardened and he would not let the Israelites go. He went back on his word (see 9:1-7).

So God said to Moses, "Get some soot out of the ovens where My people make the bricks to build the Egyptian pyramids. Throw the soot in the air; it will go across the whole nation of Egypt and cover the people with boils." Some say the boils may have been anthrax or smallpox; we don't really know. But all the people in the land, except for the Israelites up in the hills of Goshen, were covered with boils. They scratched, they itched, they hurt; it was terribly painful. Even Pharaoh had them! But still he said, "I won't let you go" (see 9:8–12).

So God brought upon Egypt a seventh plague—a plague of hail. This was hard for Pharaoh to accept, which is understandable, because in northern Egypt they get only about one inch of precipitation per year. Any kind of serious rainstorm, let alone one with hail, was practically unheard of. There was no storm in Goshen, where the Israelites lived. But the hail in Egypt destroyed the flax and barley harvest. And because it was probably a wet year, they had a bumper crop.

This time Pharaoh said, "I have sinned; I am in the wrong. If you will pray that the hail stops, I'll let the people go." So Moses came and prayed, the hail stopped and again Pharaoh's heart was hardened and again he said, "No, I'm not going to let you go" (see Exod. 9:13–35).

So God brought upon them still another plague—of locusts. The locusts were so thick you could not see the ground. They ate up everything that was left that the hail didn't destroy. Talk about a devastated land! Again Pharaoh was warned, and again he refused. So the locusts came upon the land and ate up everything. And Pharaoh's heart was still hardened (see 10:1–20).

A very significant point about this plague is that God instructed Moses to say to Pharaoh, "How long will you refuse to humble yourself before [God]?" (10:3).

Finally, the ninth plague, the last one we're going to look at in this chapter, came upon Egypt. A plague of darkness came over the land for three days. Again, some commentators speculate that the winds which sometimes blow across the Sahara into Egypt blew up enough dust and dirt to literally block the sun. How God chose to do it doesn't matter to me. But it happened exactly at Moses' command, and it ceased as soon as Pharaoh asked him to take the darkness away. But Pharaoh's heart was still hardened and he would not let the children of Israel go. He promised and went back on his promise (see 10:21-29).

From the story of these plagues, we can learn two things that God wants to set us free from: judgment and bondage. This is the answer to how we can be free, just as the Israelites eventually became free.

FREEDOM FROM JUDGMENT

All the plagues are examples of God's judgment, so the most basic lesson from this story is this: how to be nailed by God's judgment, or how to escape it. If you want to be nailed by God's judgment, just act like Pharaoh; if you want to escape it, act like Moses. What could be simpler? But there are four basic observations I want to make about God's judgment.

First, God's judgment is the worst kind of judgment. You may be judged wrongly by your friends or harshly by your enemies. You may be judged by people in church, the kids at school or even by a court of law. But all those things are nothing compared to the judgment of God.

If we can learn anything from the ten plagues of Egypt, it is that the judgment of God is relentless, ruthless and unstoppable. You can't refuse it, deny it or get away from it. Pharaoh tried, but he couldn't, because the judgment of God is the worst. Don't be afraid of other people judging you, or even the judgment of a government, a church or a school. Those judgments are important, but they're nothing compared to the judgment of God.

The second observation is this: God's judgment will come. For those who refuse to humble themselves before the almighty God, it's just a matter of time before some plague takes them down. Pharaoh learned that the hard way. I've met other people who seemed to be learning it the hard way too—and at one point in my life I think I was learning it the hard way.

The third observation is this: God's judgment does not come all at once. Sometimes it comes in natural ways—a little here, a little there. Through the ten plagues, God's judgment didn't happen all at once. He could have gone straight to the tenth plague first and ended the whole thing, but He didn't. Maybe He does it that way to allow us time to repent.

So far, this has all been bad news. The last observation I want to make is a bit more positive: You can escape God's judgment. Moses did. Israel did. The land of Goshen did. The big question is, how? The answer is in Exodus 10:3 in the message God gave through Moses and Aaron to Pharaoh: "How long will you refuse to humble yourself before me?" That is the consummate question asked of every sinner on the planet: How long will you refuse to humble yourself? How long will you go on like this? How long will you try to do it yourself? How long will you think you can be in charge of your life? How long will you try to find freedom in this very dependent world? How long are you going to act like you can set yourself free? How long do you think you can avoid God's judgment? But those who humble themselves before God will find grace and mercy.

This truth came home to a pastor friend of mine named Chuck Tyree, who took a trip a while ago to the Sudan, a country with many groups who have been notorious in the past for severely persecuting Christians—torturing and killing those who refuse to convert to Islam. Hundreds of thousands of people fled for their lives. Chuck visited a camp with 25,000 Sudanese refugees, hearing story after story after story. He said he couldn't help but have a lump in his throat and a tear in his eye all day long.

He met one group of men who had all been through the same torture. Their persecutors didn't want to leave scars on their bodies so they put these men in a tank with water up to their chins. They were left there until they renounced Christ or lost consciousness from exhaustion and drowned. They stood there in their own excrement, hour after hour, for five days. Finally the water was released and they escaped.

He met another man whose legs were crippled from

merciless beatings because he wouldn't renounce Christ and become a Muslim. Chuck interviewed kids who had no parents, parents who had no kids and hundreds of people who had been driven from their homes.

But in the midst of all those stories of suffering, one astounding thing stood out. "I couldn't believe how happy those people were," he said. "I have seldom ever seen worship, praise and rejoicing like I saw among those people. And I thought to myself, *What are they rejoicing about? Their loved ones are dead, and they are left with nothing!* Then I thought, *What's my problem? I've got everything, but I don't rejoice like these people.*

"After seeing the same thing from person to person, I started really wondering what was going on," he said. "Through a translator I asked the guy with the busted-up legs, whose wife and kids were all dead, 'Why are you so happy?'" Chuck said his answer was, and I quote, "You don't have to choose between your happiness and God's happiness. Make God happy and you can be happy."

What kept Pharaoh from humbling himself before God? He thought it was a choice between his happiness and God's happiness. And he chose his own happiness. What keeps someone from coming to God when He says, "How long will you refuse to come to Me?" They think it's a choice between their happiness and His happiness.

But this man in the refugee camp says we're not even asking the right question. If you turn to God and make Him happy, He'll take care of your happiness. And Chuck said it was so powerful to hear a man who had nothing say, "I'm happy because I have the Lord, because I've escaped the most powerful judgment that will ever come to a human being. Maybe I've been judged severely by other humans, but the final judgment is in my favor."

This man had laid hold of the truth of freedom from

judgment like most of us never have. "How long will you refuse to humble yourself before the Almighty?" That's what Pharaoh was asked. And I wonder sometimes, how much of Pharaoh is in us?

FREEDOM FROM BONDAGE

The second thing we learn from the first nine plagues is that God wants to set us free from bondage. Of course, this passage is all about bondage, isn't it? Bondage can happen in many ways. The Israelite people were in bondage to the Egyptians.

But the Egyptians were enslaved to their religion. And God turned it around so that the very things they worshiped led to their destruction.

We know people can be in bondage to drugs, alcohol, gambling, pornography—all kinds of addictions. In fact, those who work with addicts in my church say that a lot of people have addictive problems, but they just won't admit it. It's hard to admit you're in bondage. And what is probably the worst kind of bondage is right here in this passage. Did you pick it up? The worst kind of bondage is not slavery or drugs or alcohol. The worst kind of bondage is self-bondage.

What was Pharaoh enslaved to, if not himself? And when someone is enslaved to himself, his destruction is sure. Pharaoh's destruction happened because he was enslaved to his own ego, his own plans, his own dreams, his own thoughts. That is the worst kind of bondage.

A person in bondage tends to make vows and then break them. Isn't that just like an alcoholic? "I'm not going to drink anymore—I promise." Or someone who smokes says, "I'm not in bondage to cigarettes. I can quit any time I want." And he does—for a few minutes. It's just like the old joke, "It's easy to quit smoking; I've done it a million times!"

If you find yourself making vows—"I won't do that again,

I won't say that again"—and breaking them, guess what? You're in bondage. A sure sign of bondage is when you can't stop, you can't start, you can't change. That's where Pharaoh was. How can such bondage be broken? The answer is in what Moses and Aaron said to Pharaoh: "How long will you refuse to humble yourself before the Almighty?" (see Exod. 10:3).

A third thing we learn about bondage is this: Everyone is in bondage to someone or something. Look through the text: We see Pharaoh in bondage to himself, the Egyptians in bondage to their religion and even Moses in bondage—to his God. In just the same way, the apostle Paul called himself a bondslave of Jesus Christ. You're going to be in bondage to one thing or another, and the worst is to be in bondage to yourself. The only way to be set free is to be in bondage to God, the only Being who is truly free.

If you don't believe that we are always in bondage to something, take another look at Exodus 10:3. At the end of the verse, Moses and Aaron say to Pharaoh, "Let my people go [i.e., freedom], that they may serve me [i.e., bondage]." It's just as that old Bob Dylan song says: you "Gotta Serve Somebody." And the only way to be free from bondage to self, to a drug, to a religion or to anything else, is to be in bondage to God.

Let yourself be enfolded by Him; grasp onto Him. After all, He's the only one who is truly free. He's the only one who can free us from ourselves and our own sinfulness.

When my friend Chuck Tyree was in that Sudanese refugee camp, a little boy came and stood next to him everywhere he went. "He shadowed me all day long for two days," Chuck said. "He didn't say anything. He just stood there. Finally I got the translator to ask him, 'Why do you keep following this man around?' The little boy answered, 'My parents and all my brothers and sisters have died. Everybody else gets to stand by somebody, and I don't have anybody to stand by. Would it be

OK if I stood by you while you're here? It makes me feel safe.'
I just hugged that little guy. I wanted to take him home. All
he needed was somebody to stand by."

As I heard that story I was reminded of this text. The only
way to escape judgment, the only way to be free from bondage,
is to stand by the Lord. It's your only hope, the only way
out, the only source of freedom. It's the only way to escape
God's judgment. That little boy was looking for security and
freedom, and his best hope was to stand by a man who was
free, someone who was stronger. It's your only hope too. Stand
by the Lord.

Chapter 12

Will You Escape
the Judgment of God?

Years ago I had a yellow Labrador retriever named Ginger. She was a very good dog, but when she was about two years old, I discovered that she had a serious deficiency. I was walking near a body of water with my brother and a friend of his who had a black Labrador. Ginger and the other dog ran toward the water and jumped in. The black Lab began swimming like a fish; Labradors are bred to be water dogs. But my dog got in the water and just thrashed around, paddling like she was going to drown.

This other guy started laughing at my dog, which really offended me. "What's wrong with your dog?" he asked. "You've got a Labrador that can't swim!"

"Well," I replied, "she's never been in the water before." It was true—she had never been in the water before—but I was just making excuses. It was sad to have a two-year-old Labrador—a dog bred for the water—that couldn't swim.

It reminds me of the human predicament. How sad it is that mankind is created to have a relationship with God, yet mankind is detached from God. What we were created to have, the whole reason for our existence, is missing in most people's lives. In fact, to reveal the detachment between people and

God, all one needs to do is talk about theology and doctrine. People's eyes start to glaze over and they say, "What does this have to do with reality? What does this have to do with my life?"

They don't understand that theology is God's reality. It's where God lives. Theology is God's logic. That's who He is and how He thinks. But when I talk in these God-concepts, I see people's eyes glaze over and I realize they don't care. Oftentimes I have been the same way—I don't care either. It just shows how detached we are from God and God's reality.

The tenth plague of Israel is a theological concept. God performed this miracle as an event in history, but it is very clear by the way He did it that He was also revealing truth about Himself and His character to mankind. God wants us to understand His reality and learn to know Him, which was what we were created for.

The concept we learn from the tenth plague can be summarized in a single sentence: God's judgment is coming upon everyone, but some will escape. By presenting it through a dramatic, historical "visual aid," God takes this truth about Himself and puts it on a low shelf so everyone can reach it. There's no excuse; anybody can understand this concept because He has put it into a real-life situation.

THE STORY

Here's what happened: God said to Moses, "The tenth plague I'm going to bring upon Egypt is the last. It will cause Pharaoh to let the children of Israel go. My death angel will swoop down over Egypt and kill the firstborn son in every house, whether king or slave. Even the firstborn of the livestock that are left in the land will be killed. But there is a way you can escape. If you follow what I command you now, you and all Israel can escape the judgment of My death angel.

"From now on, I want you to consider this month the first month of your year—that's how significant this event is. On the tenth day of the month, I want the head of every household to pick out the nicest yearling lamb he has, one without any blemish, and on the fifteenth day I want him to slaughter it and drain the blood into a bowl. Then take a bunch of hyssop branches, dip it into the blood and smear it over the top and sides of the door of your house.

"Then I want you to take the lamb, roast it, sit down with the whole family and eat it. Everything that you don't eat, I want you to burn up. Eat that lamb, all of you, and eat it fast. Eat it with bitter herbs to show the bitterness of your slavery. Eat unleavened bread with it, to show the haste in which you are eating—you won't even have time to let the bread rise!

"I want you to take your robes that you usually have hanging down to your ankles and tuck them into your belts like do when you are running—again, to show that you are doing this quickly—because as soon as you eat, I am going to deliver you. Every house that has the blood on the top and sides of the doorposts, I will spare the firstborn in that house. Every house that doesn't have it, even if he is an Israelite, I will kill the firstborn son. That's my judgment." Then Moses told all of Israel what God commanded them to do (see Exod. 11:1–12:28).

Let's look in the Bible and pick up the story from there:

At midnight the Lord struck down all the firstborn in the land of Egypt, from the firstborn of Pharaoh who sat on his throne to the firstborn of the captive who was in the dungeon, and all the firstborn of the livestock. And Pharaoh rose up in the night, he and all his servants and all the Egyptians. And there was a great cry in Egypt, for there was not a house where someone was not dead. Then he summoned Moses and Aaron by night and said, "Up, go out from among my people, both you and the people of

Israel; and go, serve the LORD, as you have said. Take your flocks and your herds, as you have said, and be gone, and bless me also!"

The Egyptians were urgent with the people to send them out of the land in haste. For they said, "We shall all be dead."

At the end of 430 years, on that very day, all the hosts of the LORD went out from the land of Egypt. It was a night of watching by the LORD, to bring them out of the land of Egypt; so this same night is a night of watching kept to the LORD by all the people of Israel throughout their generations. (Exod. 12:29–33, 41–42)

The annual celebration of this event is known as Passover. As I said before, in this event God not only delivered His people from slavery, but He did it in such a manner as to impress a significant truth upon the Israelites' minds—and upon ours, as well. That's why He said to Israel, "Practice it from now on in all of Israel, every year" (see 12:24-27).

What truths is He revealing here? What concepts do you need to take from this story? I have identified three main points. Like I said, this is on the low shelf. You need to grab this for yourself.

1. YOU NEED PROTECTION

The first thing we learn from this event is: You need protection to escape God's judgment. Notice Exodus 12:30: "For there was not a house where someone was not dead." In every single household there was either a dead lamb or a dead boy. God said they could have protection for their little boy by sacrificing a little lamb. That's the way God designed it and by doing so He was revealing something about Himself and His judgment.

Why did God do this? Why didn't He just judge the Egyptians? Why did He require the life of a perfect little lamb from every Israelite's herd? Why did so many Egyptian children have to suffer like this? What was God doing here? God was revealing something about Himself.

In our day and age, especially in America, the popularized view of God is the big Grandpa in the sky who is nice to everybody. He's kind, gentle, generous, loving and merciful, but we totally forget all the other qualities of God, such as His holiness, justice and truthfulness. We paint a picture of God so that we can manipulate Him and imagine Him to be happy with us no matter what we do.

That view of God is a fictitious character—no more real than Bugs Bunny! That's not who God has revealed Himself to be. Right here in the face of that, God says, "My judgment is coming on everybody. Unless you have a sacrificial lamb, My judgment is coming on you too. If you're going to escape it, you need protection from Me."

The popularized view of God, on the other hand, is very much missing the point. I think that's why in those places in Scripture where God directly reveals Himself—through angels, visions, etc.—people fall on their faces in fear, because they finally get it.

Some may look at a story like this in the Old Testament and say, "Well, that's the Old Testament God. The New Testament God is Jesus, who told us to love our enemies and pray for those who persecute us. It's different." Not exactly. In the New Testament, there are many passages that talk about this same kind of God. Let's take a look at just one:

> And let us consider how to stir up one another to love and good works, 25 not neglecting to meet together, as is the habit of some, but encouraging one another, and all the more as you see the Day drawing near.
>
> For if we go on sinning deliberately after receiving the knowledge of the truth, there no longer remains a sacrifice for sins, but a fearful expectation of judgment, and a fury of

fire that will consume the adversaries. Anyone who has set aside the law of Moses dies without mercy on the evidence of two or three witnesses. How much worse punishment, do you think, will be deserved by the one who has trampled underfoot the Son of God, and has profaned the blood of the covenant by which he was sanctified, and has outraged the Spirit of grace? For we know him who said, "Vengeance is mine; I will repay." And again, "The Lord will judge his people." It is a fearful thing to fall into the hands of the living God. (Heb. 10:24–31)

The last verse in this passage was the source of one of the most powerful sermons ever preached in North America, one that started a spiritual awakening throughout the continent. Entitled "Sinners in the Hands of an Angry God," it was preached before the Revolutionary War by Jonathan Edwards. Historical documents say that when people heard this sermon they shook in their seats, wept, fell down and begged for mercy from God. They finally started to see God in His reality, the truth of who He is. He's kind and merciful enough to help us if we will take His way of escape, but He declares His judgment will fall on us just like it fell on everyone in Egypt.

In the story of the Passover, God is saying, "If you don't take Me seriously, you will be surprised by My judgment." This story is God's warning to every single person; He even told the Hebrews, "Practice this every year to remind yourselves that My judgment will fall and you need protection from it." The only way you can be protected is with the blood of the Lamb. This idea, of course, carries over into the New Testament, where a multitude of times Jesus is referred to as the Lamb who was sacrificed for our sins.

2. YOU NEED CLEANSING

The second thing we learn from this story is: You need cleansing to escape God's judgment. When John the Baptist saw Jesus passing by, he said, "Behold, the Lamb of God!" (John 1:36). What did he mean? He meant the Passover lamb. He was talking about the very event we are talking about. Christ is the Passover Lamb of God who takes away the sin of the world. That's what Jesus came to earth for.

First John 1:7 says, "But if we walk in the light, as he is in the light, we have fellowship with one another, and the blood of Jesus his Son cleanses us from all sin." Here it declares that Jesus' blood is like the lamb's blood that was put on the doorposts in the original Passover. Just as that blood cleansed the Israelites from sin in God's eyes, so Jesus Christ can be our Passover Lamb and cleanse us from our sin.

When God looks at your life, He can see you clean of all injustice, lust, greed, selfishness, arrogance, pride and foolish statements. All those things can be washed away by the blood of the Lamb of God. It gives a whole new meaning and understanding to Passover, doesn't it? The judgment of God is going to come upon you, but God saves you from it.

That's what the term saved means. It doesn't just mean saved from your sins; it means saved from God. It doesn't just mean saved from the judgment of your sins; it means saved from the judgment of God, because God's judgment is coming. It's just a matter of time for everyone.

This idea is often not understood because we miss the point in the story. Let me ask you a question: What did Israel do that was wrong? It is easy to understand why God's judgment would come upon the Egyptians. They were slave drivers, they were abusive and they worshipped false gods. But the Israelites didn't. They weren't driving slaves or worshipping false gods. Why would God's judgment come upon an Israelite who didn't put the blood over his house?

God was revealing to Israel, through the blood of the lamb, that they were dirty and didn't know it. They were just as much sinners as the Egyptians. Why? Because they weren't perfect.

God views humans as either perfect or guilty. You're one or the other. Since no one is perfect, then we're all guilty—guilty of infractions against almighty God and His justice, holiness and truthfulness. Because of that, we are going to be judged, and the only way we can be protected, the only way of escape, the only way to be clean, is the blood of the Lamb.

Even in the New Testament, the message is the same: It's the blood of Jesus, the Lamb, that cleanses us from sin. First John 1:7, which I quoted earlier, is actually written to Christians. Sometimes as Christians we get dirty and we don't know it; we break fellowship with God. We need to renew that fellowship through confession.

A woman whom I will call Sharon moved to our area a few years ago and began attending the church. She told me that she had attended church all her life and even taught Sunday school. "But it wasn't until I was here for a couple of years," she said, "that I began to understand the truth about who God was and who I am. For the first time in my life, I realized I'm a sinner! I never thought of myself as a sinner. I never did anything bad. I never hurt anybody. I never intentionally tried to be mean or anything. How could I be a sinner? But I started to realize I was. I was dirty and I didn't know it."

Almost every weekend people come to my church and, as far as they know when they walk in the door, they are on the up and up with God and everything's fine. But by the end of the sermon, they come forward telling me, "I'm dirty and I didn't even know it." God pushed a button in their hearts and revealed a sin they needed to confess. They say, "I'm clean in every area but one. I'm not letting God clean that up. Now God has been talking to my heart. Will you pray with me?"

Is it possible that you are dirty and don't know it? Maybe there is something that God is trying to show you about yourself—something that keeps breaking fellowship between you and Him. Ask Him, "Lord, I know You are the Judge. I know You don't put up with sin. Is there something in my life that I need to confess?"

One of the most comforting verses I know is First John 1:9. It says, "If we confess our sins, he is faithful and just to forgive us our sins and to cleanse us from all unrighteousness." What a great verse! I need that verse, don't you? You might even need it right now. Take a bath in the blood of the Lamb.

3. YOU NEED A SUBSTITUTE

The third thing we learn is this: You need a substitute to escape God's judgment. The Passover story has the heart of the gospel in it. The lamb that the father of the house was to slaughter and eat was a substitute in place of his firstborn son. God was saying, "If you sacrifice an unblemished lamb, I will accept that as a substitute, a payment for my judgment rather than killing your firstborn son."

The idea of substitution is extremely important for us to understand, because if you are counting on God to be nice to you because you are pretty nice, you don't understand the Scriptures at all. The Scriptures do not ever say that God is "nice." He is loving; He is kind; He is generous; He is gentle, but He is not "nice." God is not "nice" to some people and "mean" to others; He is just with everyone. If He let anybody off the hook, He'd be unfair; He'd be unjust. God won't do that. He will not compromise. He's going to judge, and unless there is a substitute to take your place, then you will be judged.

That's the whole basis of Jesus Christ dying on the cross as our substitute. There's no better verse in the whole New Testament that explains this than Second Corinthians 5:21: "He made him [Jesus] to be sin who knew no sin, so that in him we might become the righteousness of God." You can actually be made to look totally righteous in God's eyes if you let Jesus be your substitute by accepting Him as your Savior and Lord.

The great preacher Donald Grey Barnhouse was once asked by a group of students to explain how Jesus could be the substitute for their sin. He said, "It's like this. Imagine that I am a judge, so what I say is law. Into the courtroom comes my son, accused of reckless driving. The evidence against him is abundant; there is no other conclusion: He's guilty. As the judge, I declare him guilty and lay on him the strictest fine I can. Then I get down off the bench, take off my robe, walk over and pay the fine."

One of the students responded, "Dr. Barnhouse, that can't be. God just can't come down off the bench."

He answered, "Precisely. That's the whole point of the Incarnation. That's what Jesus came for. God couldn't come down off the bench so He became a man and died on the cross. He became the Lamb of God to be a sacrifice, a substitute for our sins."

If you understand this concept, you get the whole Bible. If you don't get it, you miss the whole point. Even way back in the Old Testament, He's teaching this, and it carries through to the end of the Bible. In Revelation, John portrays Jesus as "a Lamb, looking as if it had been slain" (5:6). Those who worship Him said, "You were slain, and with your blood you purchased men for God" (5:9). Have you made the Lamb of God your substitute?

Chapter 13

THE FEAR FACTOR

My father had an unusual upbringing. When he was two, his mother died from a tuberculosis plague that swept across the country. Dad was passed around to different relatives and was eventually raised by his grandparents. In his teen years, he was invited by a friend to a youth meeting at church and was led to a deep commitment to Christ.

My dad began to find his identity in Christ and his fatherhood in God. It was pretty dramatic, and it meant a lot to him because when he was eighteen, he joined the Marine Corps and fought in World War II. In a very practical way, his faith had to be lived out daily, because he was facing life-and-death situations. When he came back from the war, he married my mom, and that's how I got here.

Dad was one of the toughest guys I ever met—not mean (he was a very gentle man), but tough in the sense of being strong, faithful, dependable and enduring. I never saw my dad cry, not once. For a man who has been through a world war and a difficult childhood, it is hard to cry, I guess. Mom said she saw him cry once—when the doctor came in and told him he had a brain tumor the size of a tennis ball. She said, "His eyes filled up with tears; one rolled down his cheek and dripped onto the pillow in the hospital bed." Two days later, he died.

As tough as he was, however, my dad was known in our household as the worrier. Mom used to joke that he would worry for the both of them—and he did. He worried about us kids a lot, maybe because he had seen so many bad things happen. Maybe the uncertainty of his upbringing was the cause of it, but in a very real way, he was controlled by fear.

I think there are a lot of people like that. They may consider themselves tough, but inside they are eaten up with fear—controlled by it. Fear controls people in many different ways: There is the fear of being in a crowd, the fear of being alone, the fear of not getting enough money or of losing the money you have, the fear of criticism, the fear of being ignored, the fear of getting a serious disease—and the list goes on.

Fear can manifest itself in anger, in worry, in trying to control and manipulate situations and people, in obsessive planning, in not planning at all and even in withdrawal. In ways we may not really understand ourselves, our actions are often controlled by fear.

When God freed the children of Israel from bondage to the Egyptians, He knew they were still in just as much bondage as before—a bondage to fear. And when God looks at the church today, He sees us free from our sins by the blood of Jesus Christ, but often still in bondage. God wanted to set Israel free from that bondage, and He wants to set us free as well.

The crisis at the Red Sea (see Exod. 13:17–14:31) was certainly a cause for fear: The Egyptian army was coming to destroy them! They appeared to be trapped—and all because they camped where the Lord told them to camp. Many of us have been in that kind of situation, where we follow God's leading and end up in a pinch, and we cry out, "God, why are You doing this?"

God wants to set us free, but until we fully turn to Him and surrender even our fears to Him, we are going to be in bondage, dominated by fear. That's what we learn in this passage. There are three basic principles to look at. But before we do that, let's review the story.

When the children of Israel left Egypt, God told Moses not to take the normal route to Canaan, which ran north of the fork of the Red Sea. Instead, He led them south—by a cloud in the daytime and a pillar of fire at night, the Scriptures tell us (see Exod. 13:17–22). This route meant that sooner or later they were going to have to cross the Red Sea to get to Mount Sinai, where God would give them the Ten Commandments.

But as they camped near the shore of the Red Sea, they looked behind them and saw the Egyptian army coming. They were trapped!

> When Pharaoh drew near, the people of Israel lifted up their eyes, and behold, the Egyptians were marching after them, and they feared greatly. And the people of Israel cried out to the Lord. They said to Moses, "Is it because there are no graves in Egypt that you have taken us away to die in the wilderness? What have you done to us in bringing us out of Egypt? Is not this what we said to you in Egypt: 'Leave us alone that we may serve the Egyptians'? For it would have been better for us to serve the Egyptians than to die in the wilderness." And Moses said to the people, "Fear not, stand firm, and see the salvation of the Lord, which he will work for you today. For the Egyptians whom you see today, you shall never see again. The Lord will fight for you, and you have only to be silent." (14:10–14)

You probably know the rest of the story: God moved the pillar of cloud between the Israelites and Egyptians and told Moses to raise his staff over the sea. All night long, as the Egyptians were held at bay, God sent "a strong east wind" (14:21) to divide the waters so the Israelites could cross over on dry land. When the Egyptians tried to pursue them, the Lord threw the army into confusion and they ended up stuck in the dry seabed, with the wheels of their chariots broken.

God told Moses to raise his staff over the sea again, and "The waters returned and covered the chariots and the horsemen; of all the host of Pharaoh that had followed them into the sea, not one of them remained" (Exod. 14:28). The Bible says that when the Israelites saw all this, "the people feared the Lord, and they believed in the Lord and in his servant Moses" (14:31).

WHAT WE CAN LEARN FROM THIS STORY

We could spend quite a bit of time talking about this "east wind" and where they actually crossed in the Red Sea and how deep the water really was. Some speculate that it was very shallow, so that's how they got across. But if it was that shallow, how did it drown the whole Egyptian army?

Some even suggest that it was just a fictitious story used to teach a lesson, but if that were true the Hebrew text would have been written in a whole different style. It is clearly presented as historical fact. There are too many details about this story that make it difficult to explain away. I think it actually happened as the Scripture says. Debating it is a waste of time.

It is true, however, that this story has a lesson. Just as the story of the Passover lamb contains a concept that runs through the whole Bible, so the crossing of the Red Sea has a deeper meaning behind it. There are principles here, principles that apply just as much today as they did back then. This story tells us that as the people of God, we need to follow God— and the only thing that prevents us from doing that is our own fear.

Just as God looked down on Israel and saw their problem with fear, He looks down on the church today and says, "I've delivered you, but you're still so fearful that it dominates you. I don't want My people dominated and in bondage, so I'm going to set you free." But He might have to lead you to a Red Sea experience to get that to happen. We learn three different things here that I want to point out.

1. STAND ON HIS PROMISES

The first lesson is in Moses' response to the people when they accused him of leading them into a deathtrap: ""Fear not, stand firm, and see the salvation of the LORD, which he will work for you today" (Exod. 14:13). The first thing you need to do to deal with the fear in your life is to stand firm on God's promises. What did Moses mean by that statement?

Obviously, he didn't mean to literally stand there, because then the army would have killed them! He meant stand firm in your convictions—on the promises of God, on what God has said. He said to them, "Stand firm for today you will see the Lord deliver you." He was telling them that, when facing a fearful situation, there comes a point at which they needed to make a clear, conscious decision to stand against the worry and anxiety.

Anyone who says that he's never afraid is either not in touch with his emotions at all or is living in denial. Or maybe he's gotten to the place that Moses had, because it doesn't look like he was afraid here. And even if he was, he still made the right decision by saying, "I'm going to stand firm." And he challenged the Israelites to do the same.

If fear doesn't lead us into denial, it may put us in a defensive mode, where we end up shouting or getting mad. But most often when you or I are afraid, we just get very, very attentive: "I need to figure this out. There's got to be a way out of this; there's got to be a creative alternative."

This is what we call worry or anxiety. It keeps you up at

night. You're worried about the big meeting, about losing your job, about your financial situation. Maybe you're worried about someone being mad at you, or you're mad at someone else and you stay up and think it through, and think it through, and think it through again. Overattentiveness—that's what worry is.

Sometimes we excuse our worry by saying, "I'm just trying to process this." But those who say such things are not standing firm; they're really running—desperately running, trying to find an answer. Moses is saying to stand firm and say, "The Lord is going to deliver me; I'm trusting in His promises." That's what he's challenging us to do.

What does it mean to stand firm? Maxie Dunnam tells the story of a Methodist patriarch in Estonia named Alexander Koom. He had been a church leader under the reign of Stalin. Government officials asked Koom to join his denomination with several others and form a single church. In other words, they wanted control of the churches. Koom could see what was going on, and he refused.

The officials said, "You Christians are always taking the hard way out. This could be easy. You just join up with all these other denominations and be one group. It would be state-run; we would take care of you and handle things for you." When Koom still refused, the officials said, "What are you, crazy? You've got to do this. What difference is it going to make?"

Koom responded, "If you give me a rope and you tell me to go hang myself and I go and do so, it's my responsibility. But if you take a rope and you hang me, you're responsible." [xii]

In Alexander Koom's mind, either you stand firm or you hang yourself. That is how fear works: it doesn't hang you; you hang yourself with it—or you stand firm. That's why it is so crucial to deal with the fears in life, whether fear of financial ruin, or marital problems, or bad things happening to the kids. You can either stand firm or worry and fret until you hang yourself.

Moses said to the Israelites, in effect, "Either we learn to stand firm in the Lord, or we are all going to die." It would be their responsibility if they didn't trust the Lord. God has given you and me a tremendous responsibility to deal with our lives in a right way. Sometimes He leads you to a test, with a wall of water in front of you and the Egyptian army at your back. You are caught in the middle; what are you going to do? Stand firm. If you don't, you are going to drown.

2. BE STILL

The second step is in Exodus 14:14, where Moses says to the Israelites, "The LORD will fight for you; you need only to be still" (NIV). Again, I don't think he was literally meaning "stand still," because the Egyptian army was coming their way. He meant they should stop speaking—yakking and complaining, acting like they had to do all this by themselves. When God tells us to "be still," He is addressing our heart issues, our mental attitudes, our way of looking at the situation.

After over thirty years of being a Christian, I have learned that the way to be still, the antidote to fear, is prayer. As it says in First Peter 5:7, "Casting all your anxieties on him, because he cares for you." What a tremendous promise!

The Scriptures are full of promises like that, which only goes to show that if you want to stand firm and be still, you have to know God's Word. You have to have something to stand on, something to still your heart, and the promises of God will do that. And giving your fears over to God in prayer is the only way to be still. You can talk to a lot of people and get them to sympathize with you, but Moses' answer is just "Be still." If he were writing in modern English, he might say, "Shut up, calm down and look to the Lord."

And notice what he says is the reason we should be still:

"The LORD will fight for you." Why are these people all shaken up, but Moses is calm and still in his heart? The difference was that Moses took the promises of God personally and said, "The Lord is going to fight for me." Somehow, though, the people did not believe that the Lord would fight for them.

Churches are full of people like that today. They go to church every Sunday, but when it comes down to a business deal, or the house, or money, or the kids, do they really believe that the Lord will fight for them? They should, because it is the only way to deal with fear.

If you are truly the Lord's, He will fight for you. Moses took that promise personally; he believed it. The Israelites didn't. It is possible to go through all of the motions, the rituals of Christianity, and forget that you now belong to the Lord. He bought you with His Son's blood on the cross. You don't have to fight your battles: The Lord will fight for you.

It is easy to forget this truth. The Lord had just delivered the Israelites from Egypt and already they were forgetting. I think the Lord has had to give me a lot of lessons in this because sometimes I get so fearful.

Years ago I was running a youth ministry on Friday nights, and a few hundred kids would come out. One big guy about my age showed up drunk one night. He was giving the girls a hard time, so I took him in the back room and tried to counsel with him. He didn't like what I was saying, so he turned off the light and began to punch me. I was being tested about fear!

I protected myself a bit, but a number of punches got through. I tried to live out the principle that the Lord will fight for me, so I cried out, "Lord, help!" It was like God hit this guy with a brick. He stood up, turned the light on and began to weep, and we began to talk. Twenty years later he called me on the phone, still apologizing for that night.

When we were planting a church, many were saying that

we didn't need another church in this community and that they didn't understand why I was doing it. Some said I was far too young (I was twenty-eight) and inexperienced to plant a church. They said starting the church in our house would never work. All kinds of obstacles and problems came up. I just smiled and thought to myself, *The Lord will fight for me. If this is supposed to be, He will make it happen.*

I have faced many obstacles in which I kept reminding myself and others that the Lord will fight for us. However, there have also been many times when I flunked that test. When my first daughter was in college, the finances were pretty tough and I wasn't able to contribute what I thought I should. I talked to a lot of people about it—and I wasn't simply sharing my burden; I was griping and complaining, just like an Israelite.

The Lord really convicted me: *What are you talking like this for? You are acting like I am not going to come through for you. Will I fight for you?* He did, of course. Our daughter graduated, is married now and is doing great.

Have you ever been in the same place? We do it all the time—griping and complaining is human nature. And we usually look for someone else to join in and gripe and complain with us. That's what happened to the Israelites. It was like a disease that swept through the whole community. Sometimes it sweeps through churches the same way, when instead we should say, "The Lord is going to take care of this for us; we just need to trust Him."

There are lots of things that God has brought into my life where I have had to trust Him. I once got the Epstein-Barr virus and wondered if I would ever work again, if I could even be a husband or father again. And again, the Lord reminded me, *Are you Mine? Do you belong to Me? Will I fight for you?*

I got into a little car accident at a stop sign in front of my church. I ran into the back of another car while going only a few miles per hour. The other driver looked at me and the big church and decided to sue me. Would I have to pay a big settlement? What would happen? I could have been pretty worried about the situation, but I decided to trust the Lord to fight for me. Sure enough, the judge threw the case out of court.

Over and over again, the Lord is showing me that whether it is a physical, financial, legal or personal conflict, He can fight for me. Do you really believe this applies to you personally, or is it all just religion and somehow removed from your life? God wants you to take it personally: He will fight for you. You belong to Him now, and when the Scripture says in First Peter 5:7, "Casting all your anxieties on him, because he cares for you," it means He personally cares for you. He loves you and is going to help you. That's what it means to be a child of God.

3. MOVE ON

The third thing we need to learn from this story is to move on. Notice what the Lord said to Moses in Exodus 14:15: "Why are you crying out to me? Tell the Israelites to move on" (NIV) Isn't that interesting? The Lord is telling them to stop praying! I wonder if there's anyone who thinks he prays enough; I know I don't. Yet right here in the Holy Bible, God is telling His people to stop praying and get moving. It's a clear lesson to Israel, and to you and me, that there is a time to pray and a time to move. Sometimes we get these two confused, just like Moses and the children of Israel did.

I believe there are many miracles that never happen because people never move on. If the children of Israel had stayed in their prayer meeting, there would have been no parting of the Red Sea and no destruction of the Egyptian army. They would have been destroyed. There comes a time when you can't just sit and pray anymore; it's not the answer.

I'll never forget how a professor of mine at Dallas Seminary shocked all of us by saying, "There are some things you don't need to pray about at all." He started listing promises of God and basic truths from Scripture, and said, "You don't need to pray about that; you know this. You need to move on with the truth you already know."

Part of the sickness of the people of God is that they don't move on with what they already know. Don't get me wrong—the church definitely needs to pray more! Prayer and praise times are tremendously important. But sometimes we get it mixed up, and we are sitting and praying when we should be moving on.

I saw this very graphically at one of the most fearful times in our nation—just after the September 11 attacks. I went to a prayer meeting with a group of pastors in North Jersey, and I almost jumped up and shouted when one of the worship leaders prayed, "Oh Lord, we don't know what to do."

I thought, *What do you mean we don't know what to do? We're praying and praying and praying, but isn't this tragic event a golden opportunity to spread the gospel? Isn't this the time we need to move on?*

The answer to the problems in America today is not more praise choruses or prayer meetings; the answer is for Christians to move on with what we already know. We know more than most Christians in all of church history, but we are not moving on with it. I think God is telling us today just what He told the children of Israel: "Stop crying out to Me and move on."

It's time to take the hill. We need to move out or we are done for. We can have our religious huddles and lick each other's wounds over all the tough times we are having, but it's not going to make any difference. Never once in Scripture are the people of God told to retreat. They are always told to move on.

A beautiful example of this is Todd Beamer, who was on the plane that went down in Pennsylvania on September 11, 2001. After praying with an operator on the phone, he said, "Let's roll." He prayed and then he moved on. There is a time to pray and a time to move on—to take the step of faith and do what God told you to do. As a result, Todd's story still has an impact on people. And your story will too, if you are the kind of person who can move on.

No one can escape the difficult circumstances of this life. Nowhere in the Bible does it say that everything will be perfect. You are going to face some hard, fearful things—just like me, just like Moses, just like the children of Israel. So what are you going to do?

Why don't you decide right now what you are going to do? Stand firm, be still and move on. Then you will see miracles happen.

Chapter 14

IF I FOLLOW GOD,

WHERE WILL HE LEAD ME?

I've shared Christ with many different people, and I've hardly ever talked with someone who didn't have one question at the forefront of his mind. Some form of this question is a major stumbling block to faith for many people. The question is, *If I follow God, where will He take me?*

Will He take me to a place where I can't have fun anymore? Will He take me away from my friends? If I follow God, will He make me be a missionary? (Surely you've thought of that one!) Will He put strict rules on my life? Will He hurt me or my loved ones?

Everyone asks these kinds of questions. The children of Israel were no different; even Moses was no different. It is the big question of humanity: If I follow God, what's it going to be like? These questions have kept many people from becoming Christians. They even cause many Christians to follow God cautiously, at a distance—always afraid of what He may demand of them, rather than embracing everything God brings into their lives.

On the other hand, the more you understand about God and the basic principles of following Him, the easier it is to trust God. And when you follow God closely, He can bring into your life joy, fulfillment, maturity, purpose and meaning like never before. That's what we can expect from studying the example of Moses and the people of Israel: a complete change in the way we follow God.

Chapter 15 of Exodus has three distinct principles that can help us learn to walk closer to God. Let's take a look at the story.

A PRAISE FESTIVAL

After experiencing what is probably the greatest miracle in all of human history—the parting of the Red Sea, walking across on dry land and the drowning of the Egyptian army—Moses and the children of Israel were so excited that they had a huge celebration. I guess we could call it a praise festival. In fact, Moses wrote a song for the occasion, which is recorded in Exodus 15. Can you imagine 2 million-plus people praising and thanking God for His deliverance? This makes our present-day music festivals seem like nothing.

Can you get a flavor of it all? No more working in the hot sun all day under the slave driver's whip. No more chains. No more climbing up and down pyramids. No more abuse of your women and children. You're free! As Martin Luther King, Jr., would say, "Free at last, free at last, thank God Almighty we're free at last!"

Moses' older sister Miriam was so excited that she started singing the chorus to Moses' song over and over again. All the women began to dance with Miriam, twirling and skipping and banging tambourines. And who can blame them? A bunch of slaves just won out over the meanest, toughest army in the world. It was absolutely impossible, but God made the impossible happen. Praise the Lord! (see Exod. 15:1–21).

"WHERE IS THE WATER?"

They went to bed worn out, but happy and excited. When they got up the next morning, they found that God had made things very simple for them. They were simple slaves, so He made following Him simple: He made a pillar of fire at night and a cloud by day for them to follow. If the fire or cloud moves, you move; if the fire or cloud stops, you stop. Simple folks, simple plan. Which just goes to show that God will meet you where you are.

In the morning, the cloud started moving, and led them into the desert of Shur. They headed out across the sand with all their livestock and luggage. By the end of the first day they had no water. And so the second day they headed out, with nothing but sand as far as the eye could see. By the end of the second day they were getting pretty thirsty.

On the third morning they took off across the sand dunes for hours until, finally, they came to an oasis—water! But then they discovered it was "bitter," or undrinkable. This was about as much as they could take, and they started griping and complaining to Moses. "Moses, what did you bring us out here for? Where is the water to drink?" (see Exod. 15:22–24).

What did Moses do? What he always did: He cried out to the Lord. "Lord, show me what to do." God showed him a piece of wood and told him to throw it into the water. It was probably somewhat like when Aaron touched the staff to the water in Egypt and it all turned to blood. When Moses threw the wood in, they found that the water suddenly tasted fine! God did another miracle to supply water for the people (see 15:25).

Why did God do this? The Scripture says that it was a test, apparently to see if Moses would obey God in a pinch. Moses must have passed the test, because God responded with one of the greatest promises in the Bible:

> If you will diligently listen to the voice of the Lord your God, and do that which is right in his eyes, and give ear to his commandments and keep all his statutes, I will put none of the diseases on you that I put on the Egyptians, for I am

the Lord, your healer. (Exod. 15:26)

Chapter 15 of Exodus can teach us a lot about following God. Just as the people of Israel had to learn some basics, so do we. And the first is found in the praise gathering at the start of the chapter.

1. REJOICE IN VICTORIES

We learn here that if we follow God, He will give us victories—victories that we never dreamed possible. Did the Israelites think it would be possible to cross the Red Sea? Did they think it would be possible to defeat the Egyptian army? But with God, the impossible becomes possible. If we follow God faithfully, He can lead us through obstacles and past barriers that we never dreamed we could overcome. But we also learn here that when we do have the victory, we need to rejoice. This is why God put a song in Moses' heart. He was teaching the Israelites about celebration—about worshipping and praising God.

I don't know about you, but rejoicing in victories was something I had to learn to do, especially in church. I didn't have to learn to rejoice in the victory of a ball team; that was pretty easy to do. But at church, it seemed to be a different thing.

Maybe it was the tradition I came from. I grew up in Minnesota, and almost everyone in my church had a Swedish or a Norwegian background. Scandinavians, as you might know, are not very emotionally expressive people. When they're happy or sad, you can't really tell the difference—in church, anyway. Maybe if they're watching the Vikings play, you can tell the difference. But when they're in church, it is hard to tell—or at least it was for me when I was growing up.

And so, when I accepted Christ as my Savior, I began to

study the Scriptures—passages like this and others—and said, "Hey, what's going on? How come nobody's singing excitedly? How come there's no praising? How come there's no clapping? How come nobody seems very excited about this?"

Then I got involved in the Jesus movement. I got saved in the early 1970s, and I was a Jesus freak. I ran around with these guys, and it was all about praising the Lord, singing, dancing, clapping, rejoicing and having all-night meetings. But after a while, I started not rejoicing there, either. That may sound funny, but if all you ever do is "party for the Lord," just one day after another of praising, you can actually get sick of it. That's where I was at one point of my life. Maybe you've been there too. But over the years I've learned to praise God.

Sometimes I come to church and see the worship team singing and praising Him, but some people are not joining in. And I think, *Either they have no victory in their lives—nothing to sing about—or they have not learned to praise Him and rejoice in Him.* Sometimes we can't praise God because we've come to the Red Sea and haven't crossed; we've chickened out. But oftentimes I think the opposite is the problem. We've crossed the Red Sea, but we're not praising the Lord. We're not thanking God for all the victories He's already brought for us.

Let me share an example from my life. In 1992, when I got the Epstein-Barr virus, I developed a new friendship with Martin Sanders, a professor at the Alliance Theological Seminary. We became friends because he had the same disease. He wasn't able to work; he had headaches and infections and other problems, just as I did. And so we'd commiserate with each other.

Months and months later, I was still suffering with all these debilitating problems. I called Martin on the phone and asked how it was going. He said, "Marty, it's going great! I was prayed for and the Lord touched me. I was healed."

I said, "Oh, that's nice. Praise the Lord!"

And he started joking with me about it! (You'd have to know Martin.) He said, "Sorry, Marty, it didn't happen for you." I was rejoicing with him—really, I was. But I just couldn't help thinking after I hung up the phone, *Lord, what about me? I've been prayed for several times. I've been anointed with oil in obedience to James 5, and I'm still sick. What's the problem here?*

The Lord started to show me a whole new perspective. Instead of thanking God for health or pleading with Him to give me health, I started thanking Him for the measure of health He had given me. I realized that nobody on this earth is perfectly healthy, or otherwise they'd never die. Total health is not for any of us until we get to heaven.

So I started thanking God for the measure of health He gave me—thanking Him that I didn't have a life-threatening illness, such as cancer or heart disease. I began to thank Him for my wife, my children, my church and all the people and things He had given me. And I began to see the victories He was bringing in my life. I began to rejoice and give Him thanks for all He was doing for me, even in the midst of my sickness.

I began to understand rejoicing and worship in a whole new fashion. Things don't have to seem utterly victorious. You don't have to have some miraculous healing. God still gives miracles to people like Martin Sanders, and even you and me sometimes. But sometimes He doesn't, and the answer is still the same. Are you learning to rejoice? Are you learning to thank God for the victories He's given you?

Everyone has many things they should be praising God for. The first step He taught Israel about learning to follow Him was: Learn to celebrate, learn to worship, learn to praise God. If you can't sing a song, if you can't worship Him from your heart, there's something wrong. Either you're living in defeat— you haven't crossed the Red Sea, you've chickened out—or you just haven't learned to thank God for all He's given you.

2. GOD WILL TEST YOU

The second thing we can learn is that God will test us. Exodus 15:24 says, "And the people grumbled against Moses, saying, 'What shall we drink?'" Here's a bunch of people who three days earlier were praising God and having a wonderful worship time. Now they are grumbling. How typical, right? On Sunday you had a wonderful worship time, and by Wednesday you're living in defeat. Well, that's just what they did too.

They were grumbling, as we saw earlier, because after three days of walking through the desert, the only water they found, in a place called Marah, was bitter (see 15:22–23). This teaches us that if we follow God and we're doing everything we're supposed to do, He will sometimes lead us into bitter experiences. Why would God do that?

Exodus 15:25 explains why. It says, "There the LORD . . . tested them." God brings bitter things into our lives to test us. But why would God need to test us? A test is to show what we know and don't know, but since the Lord already knows every thought and intent of our hearts, why does He need to test us? Obviously, He does it to show us what we are like.

A while ago my wife and I were praying together about something that was really heavy on our hearts. As she was praying, she said, "Lord, help us deal with this challenge." That word challenge rang in my ear. To me, that changed everything. The Lord is not being harsh or mean when He brings these things into our lives; He's just challenging us.

When I was a little boy playing catch with my dad, he would sometimes throw one real high, so I had to reach for it. Sometimes he'd throw one low and fast, so I'd have to go down and get it. And sometimes he'd throw a ground ball. Why did he do that? He was challenging me, testing me, to help me get better at catching the ball.

My mother used to make me read a book when I wanted to go out and play. Why was she so "mean"? She was testing me, challenging me, to help me learn to read. And when I was five or six years old and in my first swimming class, the instructor taught us to dog paddle and then made us swim in the deep end. *The deep end?* I thought. *But I might drown!* Why would the instructor do that? To test me, to challenge me.

That's precisely what's going on here. God tests us, like a loving parent tests a child. The thing in your life that really bugs you, that you may even be mad at God about, is there to test you, to challenge you, to get you to grow up. You won't grow up if you aren't tested and challenged. You need to say, "OK, Lord, I'll take on the challenge. Let's go; let's grow." That's what He wanted Israel to learn, and what He wants you and me to learn. God will lead you into a test—and that's a good thing.

3. GOD WILL BRING HEALING

The third thing we learn from this story is that God will bring us to healing:

> If you will diligently listen to the voice of the Lord your God, and do that which is right in his eyes, and give ear to his commandments and keep all his statutes, I will put none of the diseases on you that I put on the Egyptians, for I am the Lord, your healer. (Exod. 15:26)

What we see here is healing by obedience. Some may argue that this conditional promise—if you obey, I'll bring healing—was only for Israel at that particular time. That is a good point; it was particularly for them. But some particular principles do translate across to us. Healing by obedience still takes place. If you follow God in obedience, it will bring healing to your life morally and healing to your land socially.

In his book *How Now Shall We Live?*, Charles Colson presents statistics that show the difference God can make in a person's life. Citing voluminous research that connects a high level of religious commitment to lower levels of drug abuse, alcoholism, crime, depression, stress and family instability, he concludes, "Medical studies are confirming that those who attend church regularly and act consistently with their faith are better off both physically and mentally." [xiii]

This, of course, does not mean that every person of faith is healthy and happy, but the statistics do make a powerful statement about the typical human condition. Obedience does bring healing; statistics bear it out.

But I think there is even more implied in the statement "I am the Lord, your healer" than that. We not only will avoid the diseases of the Egyptians (especially those brought on by an immoral lifestyle), but the Lord will actually become our healer—even in the midst of illness. This passage implies that not everyone who follows God is always going to be healthy and happy; otherwise, there would be no need for God to heal.

When I got the Epstein-Barr virus, the doctors told me, "It's your job that made you sick." Long hours of pastoral ministry had broken my system down so that the disease could take over. I was hard at work for the Lord, following Him completely, and He led me right into illness. *What's that all about? I thought He was the Lord who heals us!* Well, I had a lot to learn.

I learned that whether you're sick as a dog or healthy as a horse, the best you can be is in obedience. That's the point God is teaching the Israelites, and you and me as well. The best you can possibly be—the healthiest mentally, spiritually and emotionally—is found in obedience.

The same Lord who promised to be the Israelites' healer is still our healer today. James, in his New Testament letter, said, "Is anyone among you sick? Let him call for the elders of the church, and let them pray over him, anointing him with oil in the name of the Lord" (5:14). Take your physical problem, or even a spiritual, emotional or relational problem, and offer it up to the Lord. Lay it on the altar and say, "Lord, it's your problem now. I ask you to heal me from it, remove it or help me get through it, whatever it takes. And help me obey in the midst of it and follow You."

My brother-in-law brought this truth home to me with a story from his work as a missionary in Africa. An African man was very, very sick with something that could easily be cured with antibiotics. So my brother-in-law got him some antibiotics and said, "Here, take these. I think they'll help you feel better."

The man said, "No, I'm not ready to take them yet. My friends are coming over to pray, because it's the Lord who heals, and whether He uses the pills or not, it's really up to Him. So before I take the pills, I'm going to ask the Lord to heal me."

My brother-in-law said, "What was I thinking? The Lord can use a pill or not use a pill. I felt so rebuked. I was thinking so humanly, so mechanically, so medically, and not remembering it's the Lord who heals."

So let's ask this question again: If I follow the Lord, where will He lead me? First, He'll lead you to outrageous victories, causing you to accomplish things you never dreamed you could possibly do, and He'll ask you to simply rejoice. God will also lead you into bitter experiences. He will test you like a father, because He loves you and wants you to grow up. And then He will lead you into healing. He's the one who heals us. It's all about the Lord, not just us, and we need to come to Him and obey Him.

Chapter 15

How to Be Happy Following God

As I think of the 2 million-plus people who came out of Egypt, crossed the Red Sea and went into the desert, I like to try to imagine what it was like for a single family. There must have been at least one set of parents with a sick little child. The parents may have been a little apprehensive as they left Egypt, no matter how determined they were to follow the Lord. It's possible that, as they crossed the desert, the lack of food and water may have led to the child's death. And they probably thought, *If we had stayed in Egypt, our daughter may have lived.*

I bring up this morbid example only to help you relate to what the Israelites were going through at that point. In Exodus 16, they were grumbling and complaining, even sometimes wishing they were back in slavery in Egypt. They found it very hard to follow the Lord. Maybe you can relate. How can you be happy following the Lord when He leads you through such harsh realities?

There is, of course, an option at a time like that—you can decide not to follow the Lord. Many people don't follow the Lord because they don't believe the Lord is going to make them happy enough. They think they can make themselves happier by doing what they want to do.

One such person who obviously accepted and even promoted that way of life was Aldous Huxley, a proclaimed intellectual and skeptic. In his book *The Doors of Perception*, Huxley penned these words about life on this planet:

> Most men and women lead lives at the worst so painful and at the best so monotonous, poor and limited that the urge to escape the longing to transcend themselves if only for moments is and has always been one of the principal appetites of the soul. [xiv]

His pessimistic message is "Forget about being happy. You're not going to be happy here in this world. Nobody is." Well, I disagree with Huxley. I think you can follow the Lord and be happy. In fact, I think the Lord designed it that way. But like the Israelites, sometimes we lose sight of God's design and begin to complain. In Exodus 16, the Lord shows us what we can do about that. Let's take a look at the first three verses:

> They set out from Elim, and all the congregation of the people of Israel came to the wilderness of Sin, which is between Elim and Sinai, on the fifteenth day of the second month after they had departed from the land of Egypt. And the whole congregation of the people of Israel grumbled against Moses and Aaron in the wilderness, and the people of Israel said to them, "Would that we had died by the hand of the Lord in the land of Egypt, when we sat by the meat pots and ate bread to the full, for you have brought us out into this wilderness to kill this whole assembly with hunger." (16:1–3)

They were already saying they wanted to go back to Egypt. After all they had seen God do, they were grumbling. They were following the Lord, but they were not happy. So what did the Lord do? The Lord showed them how to be happy following Him. If you are trying to follow the Lord and find yourself tempted to grumble and complain, you're in the same boat. The tremendous truth that God taught them is exactly what you and I need to learn to do—the same thing—to follow the Lord.

What we need to learn is how to live off God's provisions, as we will see later. I don't care if you became a Christian yesterday or thirty years ago, you have to learn that, and the sooner you do, the happier you are going to be. In just these first few verses, we also learn that to be happy following God, we must give up grumbling. The Israelites had a problem with that, didn't they? Well, we do too.

If you've ever thought that seeing a miracle would give you such faith that you would never doubt or complain again, you've got proof positive right in this passage that it doesn't work. This group of people saw the most outrageous miracles in human history—the ten plagues in Egypt, the parting of the Red Sea—yet they were not happy following the Lord. If you've ever prayed, "Lord, just heal her," or "Just give us this money," or "Just cause this miracle to happen, and I promise I'll be happy the rest of my life following You," you now know that it's a bunch of baloney. It didn't work for the Israelites, so why would it work with you?

Notice what they said in Exodus 16:3: "If only we had died by the LORD's hand in Egypt!" (NIV). That doesn't mean, "I wish we were dead." It means they wanted to go back to Egypt, live long lives, eat all they wanted and eventually die there. What hung them up was their first two words. They started playing the game of "if-only." You and I do the same thing: "If only we had more money; if only I had a better job; if only I hadn't lost my job; if only I wasn't married; if only I was married."

Once you start playing the "if-only" game, you can't follow God. It just leads to grumbling and complaining. Playing the "if-only" game means you are trying to be in control and follow God at the same time, which of course doesn't work. We all fall into this habit of grumbling and complaining, of using these "if-onlys." We start second-guessing God, wondering if He's really in charge and really has a plan.

There is another thing in this passage that is easily missed if you are not looking closely. Who is not complaining? Moses! Why not? Because he's following God.

STEP 1: FOLLOW GOD

The first step to being happy as you follow God is simple: You need to follow Him! As basic as it may sound, it was something the Israelites had not learned yet. They were not happy because they were not following. If you are going to follow God, you need to make a decision, and repeat that decision over and over again whenever you are tempted to start grumbling: "I am not going to play the 'if-only' game. I am not going to second-guess God, because I'm following Him. That settles it." That's where Moses was.

If you recall, Moses was not always such a faithful follower. He had played the "if-only" game earlier, at the burning bush. He questioned what God wanted, what God was doing and how He would do it. But he got over it. So there is hope for you and me!

Grumbling is epidemic, isn't it? If you want to get a conversation started with someone, just start grumbling about something. "Boy, do you think it could get any hotter? Man, we sure need some rain. How about that game last night? Man, they stink, don't they? And those referees must be blind!" Just start griping and complaining, and everybody is your friend. It's easy, it's human nature—and it's not following God.

For some of us, it's a bad habit we've slipped into. For some it may even be a family trait. It's sad, but true. I pray that you have the grace of God to deal with this in your life, just as these Israelites needed to do, and say, "I've got to stop talking and thinking like that, because when I am, I'm not following God." Grumbling and complaining fall away when you learn to follow God with your words, your mind and your heart.

STEP 2: RECEIVE GOD'S PROVISION DAILY

The second thing God teaches Israel is in Exodus 16:11–20:

> And the LORD said to Moses, "I have heard the grumbling of the people of Israel. Say to them, 'At twilight you shall eat meat, and in the morning you shall be filled with bread. Then you shall know that I am the LORD your God.'"
>
> In the evening quail came up and covered the camp, and in the morning dew lay around the camp. And when the dew had gone up, there was on the face of the wilderness a fine, flake-like thing, fine as frost on the ground. When the people of Israel saw it, they said to one another, "What is it?" For theydid not know what it was. And Moses said to them, "It is the bread that the LORD has given you to eat. This is what the LORD has commanded: 'Gather of it, each one of you, as much as he can eat. You shall each take an omer, according to the number of the persons that each of you has in his tent.'" And the people of Israel did so. They gathered, some more, some less. But when they measured it with an omer, whoever gathered much had nothing left over, and whoever gathered little had no lack. Each of them gathered as much as he could eat. And Moses said to them, "Let no one leave any of it over till the morning." But they did not listen to Moses. Some left part of it till the morning, and it bred worms and stank. And Moses was angry with them. Morning by morning they gathered it, each as much as he could eat; but when the sun grew hot, it melted.

If we have learned anything in studying Moses and the children of Israel, it is that we need to pay attention not only to what happens to them but why. Why did God do it this way? Why didn't He have a herd of cattle wander into the camp, so they'd have enough food for months? Why didn't He provide grain for them, instead of perishable manna?

God was teaching them a principle about living with Him, a principle you and I need to learn. To follow the Lord and be happy, we must receive His provisions daily. We need to learn how to take from the Lord every day.

Let me ask you a question: Who's really well off in this world in your opinion? Are the rich well off? I've known enough people with wealth to be able to say no, they are not. Some of the richest people I have met are some of the most miserable people I have met. How about successful people—those who have achieved their goals, made their mark, done something to make a difference? I haven't noticed them being well off or happy—at least, not any happier than anyone else.

The Bible teaches that the person who is really well off is the one who learns to experience God on a daily basis, to receive provision from Him every day. With this very simplistic illustration of manna on the desert floor, God was saying to the Israelites, "Go out and gather from Me every day; I want to feed you." In the same way you and I need to have our souls, our hearts and our minds fed by God every day. Whether it's reading the Word, listening to a recording, hearing a preacher, reading a book or praying, you need to have that time of relationship with God. That's the only way you can be happy following Him.

Unless you receive from Him daily, you're going to be hungry, just like an Israelite who didn't go out and get himself manna in the morning. You're going to miss out. Maybe the reason you grumble and don't feel happy following the Lord is because you don't know how to receive from the Lord yet.

My wife and I once saw a bumper sticker with this catchy little statement (it was probably even more meaningful because it was on the back of a pickup truck): "My wife keeps saying I don't listen to her . . . or something like that." My wife thought it was really funny, but I didn't appreciate it as much as she did!

But after we both had a good laugh about that, I got to thinking, and I said, "You know, that could say, 'My God keeps saying I don't listen to Him . . . or something like that.'"

Almost on a weekly basis, the Lord says that to me: "Are you listening to Me? I'm talking to you." Does He ever say that to you when you come to church?

I believe the Lord speaks all the time in ways you and I don't even comprehend—in our consciences, in our minds, in our thoughts, in our ways, in our physical conditions, in the Bible, in the Holy Spirit speaking to us. There are so many different ways God speaks. And I think He often says, "You're not listening to Me," because we don't take the time or the discipline to go out and get the manna for that day.

Meeting with and communicating with God every day is what you need to learn to be happy following Him. The sooner you learn that, the happier you are going to be.

STEP 3: REST IN GOD'S PROVISION WEEKLY

The third step is found in Exodus 16:21–30:

Morning by morning they gathered it, each as much as he could eat; but when the sun grew hot, it melted.

On the sixth day they gathered twice as much bread, two omers each. And when all the leaders of the congregation came and told Moses, he said to them, "This is what the Lord has commanded: 'Tomorrow is a day of solemn rest, a holy Sabbath to the Lord; bake what you will bake and boil what you will boil, and all that is left over lay aside to be kept till the morning.'" So they laid it aside till the morning, as Moses commanded them, and it did not stink, and there were no worms in it. Moses said, "Eat it today, for today is a Sabbath to the Lord; today you will not find it in the field. Six days you shall gather it, but on the seventh day, which is a Sabbath, there will be none."

On the seventh day some of the people went out to gather, but they found none. And the Lord said to Moses, "How long will you refuse to keep my commandments and my laws? See! The Lord has given you the Sabbath; therefore on the sixth day he gives you bread for two days.

Remain each of you in his place; let no one go out of his place on the seventh day." So the people rested on the seventh day.

Again, we need to ask why God did it that way. God is trying to teach the principle of resting in His provision weekly. When God created the world in six days, He didn't rest on the seventh day because He was tired. God never gets tired. He rested on the seventh day to teach us this principle. Human beings are wired in such a way that every seven days they need to take a day off—a day to meditate and worship.

Many people who try to follow God don't take a day off to meditate, to rethink their lives and to reconnect with God—and then they wonder why they are not happy! We may no longer be bound by law to observe the Sabbath, as the Israelites were in the Old Testament, but taking a day to meditate and reconnect with God is a principle worth implementing. Learn to take a whole day to do that and you will never regret it.

A medical doctor named Richard Swenson makes this point in his book *Margin*. He said the pages of people's lives are all full—they have no margins. He says we need to put some margin back in our lives so that they are readable and understandable—so that our lives have a message. He adds,

> The patients who come to my office do not seem rested.
> . . . Often-used descriptives of our society include active,
> busy, driven, fatigued, tired, exhausted, weary, burned-out,
> anxious, overloaded and stressed, but seldom do you hear
> our society described as well rested. [xv]

What Dr. Swenson was trying to communicate in his book filled with research was that to take a rest is "just what the doctor ordered." We desperately need it, and often we don't recognize that fact.

In the same way, the Lord's command to Israel to rest was for their own good. They were grumbling and griping because they had never learned how to rest. Swenson concludes, "A biblically authentic and balanced life will include time to be still, to remember, to meditate, to delight in who He is and what He has made. [xvi] Too often we let the world carry us on a quest for success, and we miss all that God wants us to be by never resting.

In this incident from Exodus, God was saying, "Israel, you are not happy because you are not following, you are not listening, you are not resting." And He could say the same thing of us. That's the message that you and I desperately need to hear today.

I was thinking about what these principles should look like to us when I came across a passage in the book of John that opened it up all fresh and new to me:

> So they said to him, "Then what sign do you do, that we may see and believe you? What work do you perform? Our fathers ate the manna in the wilderness; as it is written, 'He gave them bread from heaven to eat.'" Jesus then said to them, "Truly, truly, I say to you, it was not Moses who gave you the bread from heaven, but my Father gives you the true bread from heaven. For the bread of God is he who comes down from heaven and gives life to the world." They said to him, "Sir, give us this bread always."
>
> Jesus said to them, "I am the bread of life; whoever comes to me shall not hunger, and whoever believes in me shall never thirst.
>
> This is the bread that comes down from heaven, so that one may eat of it and not die. I am the living bread that came down from heaven. If anyone eats of this bread, he will live forever. And the bread that I will give for the life of the world is my flesh."
>
> The Jews then disputed among themselves, saying, "How can this man give us his flesh to eat?" So Jesus said to them, "Truly, truly, I say to you, unless you eat the flesh of the Son of Man and drink his blood, you have no life in

you. Whoever feeds on my flesh and drinks my blood has eternal life, and I will raise him up on the last day. For my flesh is true food, and my blood is true drink. Whoever feeds on my flesh and drinks my blood abides in me, and I in him. As the living Father sent me, and I live because of the Father, so whoever feeds on me, he also will live because of me. This is the bread that came down from heaven, not like the bread the fathers ate, and died. Whoever feeds on this bread will live forever." (John 6:30–35, 50–58)

He takes the whole concept we've just studied about manna and says, "I am the bread of life; feed on me and you can live forever." The answer to it all is feeding on Jesus. You need to feed on Jesus every day, following Him, listening to Him, resting in Him. That's what the Israelites needed, and that's what you and I need as well.

Chapter 16

CHANGING NEGATIVE PATTERNS

The further along we get in the story of the Israelites in the desert, the more unreasonable their grumbling and complaining sounds. Some of them even said they wanted to go back to Egypt, which sounds pretty ridiculous. Did they really want to go back into slavery? Besides, they'd have to swim across the Red Sea to get there!

And as we see in Exodus 17, they developed a rather predictable pattern to their complaints. In fact, most people who read this chapter usually respond by saying, "Didn't we just read the same thing a few pages earlier?" And they are right!

The Israelites developed a pattern that may be somewhat like yours and mine. For most of us, there are negative things in our lives that we fight against, yet we keep repeating them; they never seem to change. This passage gives us answers to that, because it's not just history—it's history with a purpose.

> All the congregation of the people of Israel moved on from the wilderness of Sin by stages, according to the commandment of the LORD, and camped at Rephidim, but there was no water for the people to drink. Therefore the people quarreled with Moses and said, "Give us water to drink." And Moses said to them, "Why do you quarrel with me? Why do you test the LORD?" But the people thirsted there for water, and the people grumbled against

Moses and said, "Why did you bring us up out of Egypt, to kill us and our children and our livestock with thirst?" So Moses cried to the LORD, "What shall I do with this people? They are almost ready to stone me." And the LORD said to Moses, "Pass on before the people, taking with you some of the elders of Israel, and take in your hand the staff with which you struck the Nile, and go. Behold, I will stand before you there on the rock at Horeb, and you shall strike the rock, and water shall come out of it, and the people will drink." And Moses did so, in the sight of the elders of Israel. And he called the name of the place Massah and Meribah, because of the quarreling of the people of Israel, and because they tested the LORD by saying, "Is the LORD among us or not?" (Exod. 17: 1–7)

What this passage is teaching is how to take what we believe and put it into our lives, which is one of the hardest things we will ever do. Most anyone who has ever come to me for counseling ends up talking about a very predictable negative pattern that they see in their lives and that they want to change. It might involve lust, greed or selfishness; it might have to do with their marriages, their money or their jobs. But it's a pattern, and they can see it. Often they know it's sinful, that it's hurtful to them, to others and to God, but they're stuck. They can't change it.

That's exactly where the Israelites were. As you can see, they hadn't changed much. Exodus 17 sounds like a repeat of previous chapters. They were in a rut. Can you relate to that? Is there an area in your life that falls into a pattern like that? Maybe it's even an addiction in some sense; you struggle with it, but you can't change.

Notice the contrast, however, between the Israelites and Moses. Moses was not grumbling. He had changed a lot. It wasn't that long ago that he was at the burning bush, moaning, complaining and making excuses, but now he's not. What changed? How did he do it? How can we do it?

A CHANGE IN WHAT YOU FOCUS ON

One of the first contrasts we see between Moses and the children of Israel is evident in the first three verses of Exodus 17. What are the children of Israel here focused on? They are thinking of their own needs, their own desires, their own comforts. That's where most people, even those who go to church, are. It leads to grumbling, quarreling, even to testing God.

But Moses is not grumbling or quarreling, because he has a whole different focus. I use that word focus because of a word that is used three times in these first three verses: the word *why*. Moses asked them two questions: "Why do you quarrel with me?" and "Why do you test the LORD?" They answered, "Why did you bring us up out of Egypt, to kill us and our children and our livestock with thirst?"

A question that begins with *why* deals with purpose and meaning. "Why are you doing this?" is the same as asking, "What is your purpose in doing this?" And that's why I use the word focus, because it is all about purpose and meaning.

As you can see very clearly in this passage, Moses' questions show that his focus is on God: "Why do you quarrel with me?" and "Why do you test the LORD?" (In other words, "It's really God you are criticizing, not me.") And their response— "Why did you bring us up out of Egypt to make us . . . die of thirst?"—shows that their focus is on their comfort and needs.

The contrast in focus here is significant. It is the kind of difference you see when you become a Christian. Your life takes on a whole new purpose. Somehow Moses had grasped that, but the children of Israel—at least, most of them—hadn't. They didn't recognize that the goal was not just survival, not just comfort. If you're still focused on survival, comfort and happiness, you've totally missed the Christian life. You're going to end up grumbling, quarreling and even testing God, just like an Israelite.

These negative patterns in your life that you can't seem to beat are often the result of a wrong focus. They start right at the foundation of your thinking—about what you're here for and where you're going. If the apostle Paul were here, he'd say, "The Israelites are walking by the flesh, and Moses is walking by the Spirit." As he says in Galatians 5:16, "Walk by the Spirit, and you will not carry out the desire of the flesh" (NASB). Paul is saying we need to change our entire focus and follow the Spirit of God.

Focusing on God is not just the "spiritual" thing to do; it's the only way to have a true perspective of the situation. The questions Moses asked the Israelites were intended to bring them back to the real issue that their complaint was with God, not him. Oftentimes people lose the proper perspective. Whether it's criticizing or complaining about a spouse, a pastor, the government or some other authority, we need to step back and see the big picture. It's not about them; it's about God. Are you or are you not following and focusing on God?

Malcolm Muggeridge, a famous intellectual who became a believer late in life, made a profound observation which relates to this quite well. He said he often woke up in the early morning in a sort of half-conscious, half-unconscious state. He said that at those times it was like his thinking was unusually clear, and it was almost like he could objectively see his old body lying there in bed and see life with a clearer vision. Let me quote some of what he observed:

> In that sort of limbo between being in and out of your body, you have the most extraordinary confidence, a sharpened awareness that this earth of ours, with all its inadequacies, is an extraordinarily beautiful place. . . . And finally, a conviction passing all belief that you are a participant in

His purposes for His creation, and that those purposes are loving and creative and not destructive, are universal and not particular. In that confidence is an incredible comfort and an incredible joy. [xvii]

Muggeridge was saying that, as he approached the end of his life, he saw it's all about focus, about how you look at things. And if you look at it as God's creation, and that you were created and designed by Him for His purpose and His end, that changes everything. All the issues and problems we grieve about are insignificant in light of our purpose that we seek to fulfill. That was Moses' attitude as well. After all, he was an old man too.

The children of Israel were stuck in the same struggles, the same difficulties, the same negative pattern, because their focus needed to change. They were saying, "It's all about my comfort, my desires, my feelings. It's all about what makes me feel good." And Moses was saying, "No, no, no! It's about the purpose of God. That's why we're here. All my aches and pains as an old man, all my regrets, all my feelings, take second place to my focus."

All this has practical application to our own lives. I've seen people overcome persistent, predictable, negative patterns in their lives—but only when they went back to square one and said, "My focus needs to change." That's the first difference we see between Moses and the children of Israel.

A CHANGE IN WHOM YOU TEST

The second difference between Moses and the children of Israel is indicated in a word that appears twice in this story: test. Moses said to the Israelites, "Why do you test the LORD?" (Exod. 17:2). And later it says that the Israelites "tested the LORD by saying, 'Is the LORD among us or not?'" (17:7). This word was used earlier, if you remember, when the Lord "tested"

Israel at Marah (see 15:25). However, this is a flip-flop: The Lord is not testing them; they are testing the Lord.

We've all taken tests in school, right? You get a piece of paper with questions on it; you fill in the answers and hand it back to the teacher. The teachers have been trying to pass on knowledge to you; they test you to see how much you've retained. Can you imagine how stupid it would be for an ignorant student to test the knowledgeable teacher? But that's just what happened here—Israel was testing the Lord! But Moses had learned that if you want to break out of your negative patterns of living, you need to change whom you test.

This relates to an illustration C.S. Lewis used to use when he met someone who said he didn't believe in God. Lewis would take a piece of paper and say, "Suppose this piece of paper represented the entire knowledge of all mankind. Can you draw a circle on this paper to represent what you know?" How big a circle would you draw?

If you're like me, the older you get the more you realize how little you know! Lewis said that the best thing to do would be to put a tiny dot on the paper, and most people respond that way. Then he would say, "On the basis of this small sampling of all the knowledge there is, how can you believe there is no God?" How ignorant and foolish that would be!

It's just as ignorant and foolish to test God. That's the point of this story in Exodus. Far wiser it would be to test yourself! And yet I see this over and over again when I counsel people: They come into my office and tell me about their problems, which are often perpetual, predictable, negative patterns in their lives. And they blame it on someone else! "I wouldn't be like this if it weren't for my mother," or "The problem really is my spouse," or "It's all the fault of that church I went to." They spend all their time and energy pointing at and blaming someone else.

Unless I can set them free from that, I can't help them. As long as they look outside themselves for the source of their problems, they won't get anywhere. In a counseling situation, I often say, "You know, that person you're talking about is not here, so I really can't help him. But you're here, and I can help you."

What I'm trying to do is get them to look at and test themselves, instead of testing everyone else and drawing the conclusion that everyone else is wrong and bad. So fine, your father, your spouse, your church flunked the test. How about you—are you passing? How much better it would be to test yourself. Now you're getting somewhere. Now you can change and see victory over great obstacles. But not until you test yourself.

That's what Moses was trying to get these people to see when he asked, "Why do you test LORD?" I find that when people point the finger at their fathers or mothers or someone else (and admittedly, some of us didn't have the greatest fathers or mothers; we were done wrong by many different people), the one they're really pointing the finger at is God. They're mad at Him. They're disappointed in Him.

Moses hits the nail on the head: "Why do you test the Lord?" That's who you're really griping about. And often we inadvertently do that, by putting the blame on things and people and situations, when the one we're really mad at is God. After all, He led us out into this desert; He led me into this marriage; He led me into these problems. If you want to change the negative patterns in your life, you need to start testing the one who really needs to be tested—yourself. How foolish it is for the student to test the knowledgeable teacher, which is what we do when we test God.

A CHANGE IN WHOM YOU TURN TO

The third thing we can learn from Moses is that we have to change whom we turn to. We see this in Exodus 17:4–6:

> So Moses cried to the LORD, "What shall I do with this people? They are almost ready to stone me." And the LORD said to Moses, "Pass on before the people, taking with you some of the elders of Israel, and take in your hand the staff with which you struck the Nile, and go. Behold, I will stand before you there on the rock at Horeb, and you shall strike the rock, and water shall come out of it, and the people will drink." And Moses did so, in the sight of the elders of Israel.

Do you think Moses had ever seen that happen before—water coming from a stone? It was a natural impossibility. Why did God do it that way? He was showing them that if they turned to Him, He would bring about natural impossibilities. This includes those predictable negative patterns in your life that you say will never change. People look at you and say, "He'll never change"—just like water will never come out of a rock.

I've seen people change. I've seen heroin addicts quit heroin. I've seen broken marriages brought back together. It was like water from a rock—it was God. But to do it, you have to turn to God and let Him have your life. It means following Him, even into a faith situation that looks like it will never work. But if you're following God, there's no telling what could happen.

Things that are natural impossibilities can take place for those who follow God. Moses wasn't afraid to say, "Lord, You have a problem here. It looks impossible to me, and these people are ready to stone me to death. You want me to take a stick and strike a rock? All right, let's go. It's gonna look pretty stupid if this doesn't work, but that's OK, we're gonna go do it."

HOPE, INSIGHT, DECISION

If you have a negative pattern in your life, there are three things you need. First, you need hope. You've been beaten so many times by this addiction, this problem, this difficulty that you've given up. If you don't have hope that you can change, you never will change. It starts with hope. That's what I mean by having the right focus. Is your focus on the almighty God? Do you really believe that you can follow Him and He can lead you? If you've given up hope, you've lost your focus.

Second, you need insight. You need to be able to see what the issues are. And that's what it means to test yourself. Maybe you need to go to a counselor or read the Scriptures. Maybe you need to start praying and crying out for God to show you what's really wrong. Why do you keep repeating this thing that you want to change? You know it needs to be changed; it may even be hurting people you love. Why can't you change? Test yourself and get insight.

Third, you need to make a choice, just as Moses chose to follow God. Every one of us comes into these situations on a regular basis where we have a choice to make. Am I going to follow God or not? Am I going to obey Him even when it looks stupid, like striking a stick on a rock for water? Making a choice is what hangs up many people.

Over the years of my life as a Christian I've had many friends who have changed, who have been freed from patterns in their lives they never thought they could get over. I've seen dysfunctional families healed, difficult situations resolved, the chains of drug addiction broken. I've seen God do great things—truly miraculous things, like water coming out of a rock.

But I've seen others who didn't change, who fell back into old patterns and went back to old ways. Why? It's usually that third point—the point of decision. They may have focused on the Lord and had hope. They may have gotten some insight as to what the issue really was. But they wouldn't turn it over to God, so they turned back to their money, or their friends, or their drugs, or whatever.

All the stuff I've been talking about, all the things we see in contrasting Moses and Israel can be summed up in one word: humility. The humble will be exalted. The humble will be changed. Moses understood that and humbled himself before God. He humbly focused on Him, humbly tested himself rather than God and humbly did whatever God told him to do, even if it didn't seem to make sense, like striking a rock with a stick. And Moses saw miracles. He saw obstacles removed and negative patterns changed.

How about you? Do you keep hitting the wall? Are you frustrated enough? Are you ready to give in? Have you lost hope? I encourage you to focus on the Lord and receive hope, to test yourself and gain insight, to turn to God and humble yourself.

Chapter 17

Are You the Real Deal?

I was talking a while ago to a visitor after a worship service, and I asked, "How did you happen to come to our church?"

"Oh, my wife got me to come," he said. "I came and heard the singing and I saw the people joining in and giving an offering; then you preached. I said to my wife, 'Wow! These people are the real deal.'"

I wanted to poke out my chest and say, "You're right, we're the real deal. We're not just talking this stuff; we're trying to live it. We want to be fully devoted followers of Christ. Our elders, staff members and volunteers are really godly people. They are the real deal."

Moses was the real deal. It doesn't mean he didn't have faults and problems; he did fall down now and then. But, he was truly trying to follow God. Are you the real deal? There is one sure way to find out: Just see how you respond when you get attacked. That's what happened to Moses and the children of Israel in the second part of Exodus 17. And from this story we learn who is the real deal and what it means to follow God in the midst of attack.

We still have attacks today. When you talk to people about issues such as creation/evolution or abortion, you may get attacked and be called names like "right-wing fundamentalist." You may be considered unreasonable because you believe that premarital sex and homosexuality are not just "alternative life-styles" or that gambling, drinking and drug abuse are not OK.

Or you could be attacked physically, as some Christians are today. There is not a lot in the Western media about it, but attacks against believers are taking place all around the world. There were more Christian martyrs in the twentieth century than in all the previous centuries combined, and the trend continues into the twenty-first century. Many of our brothers and sisters in Christ are being abused and murdered in places like Sudan and Somalia.

We are getting more and more familiar with physical attacks in the United States as well. There have been church burnings, mostly among black churches in the South. And even the September 11 attacks had a lot to do with the fact that the United States is considered a Christian nation. But most of the attacks we suffer are a lot more subtle. I have a friend whose church bought a piece of land with a house on it. They plan to build a church on that land. The township, however, wants to tear down the house and put a road through, without paying the church anything for it. When the church complained, a township official responded, "Go ahead, sue us."

We also suffer personal attacks. Maybe you have been verbally attacked or ridiculed by a boss, a friend, a relative or even a spouse. How you deal with attacks determines if you are the real deal. You can puff out your chest and say, "Oh yeah, I am the real deal," but how you respond when you are blindsided by a friend or relative, or even someone in church, will show if it's really true.

In fact, I believe that is why God let Israel get attacked—to help them prove that they were the real deal. Many of the attacks that come into our lives are for the same reason—God is trying to prove us, to show us what kind of Christians we really are.

The children of Israel were entering into a place called Rephidim, which was ruled by the Amalekites. The Amalekites were descendants of Amalek, the grandson of Esau. You may recall from the book of Genesis that Jacob and Esau were children of Isaac. That means they were relatives of the children of Israel.

But when the children of Israel, over 2 million strong, entered their land, the Amalekites were offended that these people dared to trespass, so they attacked them. The Israelites were only passing through on the way to the Promised Land, but the Amalekites didn't seem to see it that way. Besides, they apparently thought the Israelites were an easy target. It tells us in the book of Deuteronomy that they were picking off the old people and the kids who were straggling behind (see Deut. 25:17–18).

Moses decided that something had to be done, so he called on a young man of Israel named Joshua to put together an army and fight the Amalekites in the valley of Rephidim. Meanwhile, Moses took his brother, Aaron, and his companion, Hur, to the top of a hill overlooking the valley. He carried the staff that God gave him.

Joshua and his army headed to the valley and met the Amalekites in battle. Moses took the staff in his hand—the one that he had used at the parting of the Red Sea—and raised it up in his hands. As the battle began, Joshua and his army were winning. But soon, Moses' arms began to get tired, and he couldn't hold them up any longer.

He noticed, however, that when he let his arms go down, the Amalekites started winning. So he raised his arms back up again. When his hands were up, the Israelites were winning; when his hands were down, the Amalekites were winning. So Hur came on one side of Moses and held one arm up, and Aaron, on the other side, held the other arm up until the end of the day. Joshua and the army of Israel won the battle (see Exod. 17:8–13).

The principles that God intended to teach Israel through this incident still apply to you and me today. They can help us find out how we can be the real deal and be prepared for when we get attacked. And it's going to happen: When you follow God, there will be times when He lets you get attacked. What will you do when attacks come? Moses' example teaches us three things we can do.

1. THINK CLEARLY

The first thing we can learn from Moses is his immediate response to the situation:

> Then Amalek came and fought with Israel at Rephidim. So Moses said to Joshua, "Choose for us men, and go out and fight with Amalek. Tomorrow I will stand on the top of the hill with the staff of God in my hand." (Exod. 17:8–9)

Notice that Moses didn't go into a fit of rage or allow himself to give in to fear and panic. Instead, he thought clearly. He assigned Joshua the task of getting together an army and he, as the spiritual leader of Israel, took on the task of seeking God.

I point this out because what often messes us up when we are attacked is fear and anger. We panic or we go into a rage, and we lose control. We're not thinking clearly. To be the real deal, you have to keep your head. Don't let anger or panic take you over. Of course, that can be easier said than done. It has a lot to do with knowing God's Word.

When you start trying to apply this story, however, you immediately run into a problem. How do you go to battle against somebody when, as Jesus said, you are supposed to turn the other cheek (see Matt. 5:39)? Don't we as Christians have a problem with this story? "Blessed are the peacemakers" (Matt. 5:9)—but are we going to go out and fight? How does that fit? How does it fit with "Pray for those who persecute you" (Matt. 5:44)? How do you do good to your enemies and try to kill them at the same time?

Is it just because they attacked first? If they hit you first, you can hit back? Is that what Jesus did? Did He ever fight back when He was attacked? Never once did He fight back, though He was hit, spit upon and ridiculed. He didn't attack. How about the apostle Paul? He was beaten, thrown in jail, left for dead. Did he fight back? Never once. Well then, that's not the answer.

"Well," you may say, "maybe Moses' era was a more primitive culture. By the time Jesus came, it had changed quite a bit, and in our day, of course, a lot more. That was a very primitive time—tribal warfare and that sort of thing." Really? I don't think that solves the problem.

Let me give a contemporary example. Let's say you and I are driving around one of the tougher neighborhoods of a big city at midnight, and I push you out, then take off. Then you see a group of young men walking toward you rather briskly. One pulls something out of his pocket and flips it. It's a blade. You're about to be attacked.

What do you do? Be nice? Is that going to work? You can be as nice as possible to them, but you're still going to be attacked. As the gang gets closer and closer, a police car pulls up behind you. The gang runs away and the cop asks, "What in the world are you doing here?" But you are so thankful that he is here, you don't care what explanation you have to give!

What you have experienced is an attack that was thwarted by the law, by order, by justice. Thank God that this country is not ruled by the toughest gangs or the meanest people. There is law, justice and order—and it may have just saved your life!

What I am trying to say in this story is that Jesus' words, "Blessed are the peacemakers" (Matt. 5:9), "Turn the other cheek" (see Matt. 5:39; Luke 6:29) and "Love your enemies" (Matt. 5:44), were not directed to police officers to tell them not to do their jobs. They were not directed to generals to tell them not to go to war. They were directed to people in the kingdom of God to tell them how to live their personal lives.

There is a vast difference between what the law can do and what one person can do. You should never take the law into your own hands. That's what Jesus meant when He told us to be peacemakers, to turn the other cheek and to love our enemies. But it doesn't mean there shouldn't be law, order and justice. That's what we see Moses doing here. He was seeking God's way, but he also recognized the place of law and order. That's why he sent his general, Joshua, off to war, rather than leading the army himself.

We have to make clear-thinking decisions when we are attacked, realizing that it's not up to us to enforce the law. There may be situations where the law needs to take control, and we need to call the cops or get a lawyer. But that doesn't absolve us of our personal responsibility to love our enemies. I bring this up because when we are attacked, often we get confused; panic and anger take over, and we start acting without thinking. Be careful of that. We are in the kingdom of God and under His rule.

2. WORK HARD

The second thing we learn here is that we need to respond with hard work. Exodus 17:10 says, "So Joshua did as Moses told him, and fought with Amalek, while Moses, Aaron, and Hur went up to the top of the hill." Joshua and his army fought a battle, and in case you don't know, war is ugly, mean, messy and hurtful. It was God's will that Joshua was to fight the battle, but we see very clearly in the text that the sword is not the ultimate weapon in the victory. When Moses' hands were up, the Israelites were winning with the sword. When his hands were down, they were losing with the sword. The sword wasn't winning the battle; Moses' prayers were.

The battle wouldn't have been won, however, without the sword. There still had to be hard work, messy work, ugly work. If you are going to be the real deal, you not only need to think clearly about who you are as a Christian and about what you are and are not supposed to do, but you also need a good work ethic. You need discipline and determination, because following God's will may involve messy, difficult conflict. If you are not willing to do that, I don't think you are the real deal.

This is what James meant when he said, "Faith apart from works is dead" (James 2:26). You can say you are the real deal all you want, but if, in a difficult situation, you can't trust God to help you when He gives you some work to do—no matter how ugly, messy, difficult and emotionally hard it may be—then I'm not sure you are really serious about following God. It's an issue of priorities.

A philosophy professor came to class one morning and set an empty mayonnaise jar on his desk. He looked at his students and said, "I believe this jar is empty. Do you think it is?" (When a philosophy professor asks a question like that, you know something's up!) Of course, the students said, "It's empty."

He took some rocks out of a box and started putting them into the jar, all the way to the top. He said, "Now would you say this jar is full?" They said, "Yes, it's full." He then reached into another box and pulled out a handful of little pebbles and started pouring them into the jar. The pebbles worked their way down in between the rocks. He said, "Now would you say it's full?" The students were starting to giggle by this time, and they said, "Now it's full."

But the professor wasn't done yet. He reached into another box and pulled out some sand. He poured the sand into the jar and it worked its way down into the crevices between the rocks and pebbles. He asked, "Now would you say it's full?" The class said, "Yes, it is full."

The professor responded, "This jar is like your life. The rocks are the things in your life that are absolutely essential: knowing and following God and the relationships with those you love. The pebbles are the necessities of life—the house, the job, the car. The sand is all the rest—the pleasures and trivialities of life.

"For many of you, your life is full of sand and you can't get any rocks in. Your life is so full that even the pebbles are edged out with sand. That is no way to fill up your life. The way to do it is to put the rocks in first, the pebbles in second and then put in the sand. Otherwise, we get out of whack and make wrong decisions and wrong moves."

The professor was right. We don't deal well with conflict when our lives are all sand and pebbles. One thing an attack can reveal to us is the need to reevaluate our priorities. It shows us if we are working too hard and spending too much time on things that aren't that important.

Do you want to be the real deal, to really follow God in His kingdom? Seek first the kingdom of God and His righteousness and all these other things, all the sand and the pebbles, will be added to you (see Matt. 6:33). That's what Moses did. He chose the most important thing for him to do. He said, "I'm going, not out to war, but to the top of the hill, and there I will raise my hands. I'm going to seek God."

3. PRAY TO THE END

That leads us to the third point: If you respond by praying to the end, you will see victory. When Moses was at the top of the hill, it says, "Whenever Moses held up his hand, Israel prevailed, and whenever he lowered his hand, Amalek prevailed" (Exod. 17:11).

You might notice there is no prayer given. If they didn't

pray, why not? If they did pray, why didn't they record it? I think what we learn from this is that the words aren't that important. Moses was recognizing God by lifting up his hands and staff to heaven.

The translation into our lives is that it's not about knowing how to pray the right prayer; it's about simply praying— seeking Him about our decisions, about the attacks we are facing, about whatever we do. It's about honoring Him and recognizing Him.

There are some things in life that God leaves contingent upon prayer. I wonder if the Lord is sitting up in heaven saying, "I'm ready to pour this down. I'm ready to change your life. I'm ready to bring a miracle. All somebody needs to do is ask. Call out to Me and it will come."

God has left some things contingent upon prayer. The doctors can't fix it; the intellectuals can't think it; the pastors can't make it happen. Nobody can make it happen—except God, through prayer. This should make us more serious about seeking God, especially in conflict, because some things you just can't change, you are not even supposed to try to change, but God can change them.

Do you still think you're the real deal? Over many years, I've tried with all my heart to be the real deal. This is my passion in life and will be till the day I die. Do you realize what could happen if we decided to think clearly, to work hard and to pray to the end? We would start to be the real deal, and then we would change the world.

Chapter 18

How to Keep from Messing Up

I n my life, I have been privileged to be around some very strong people—those who endured hardship, dealt with difficult situations and remained strong while others were weak. I have learned a lot from people like that.

I have also seen people mess up their lives. I have had friends who fell into sexual sin, got involved with drugs or alcohol, sabotaged relationships, destroyed their marriages or brought harm to their churches. Some got back on track, and some never did. I know how true it is that "pride goes before destruction, and a haughty spirit before a fall" (Prov. 16:18)— but I didn't need the book of Proverbs to tell me that. I have observed it myself in case after case.

I have also learned this principle from my friends who are strong: To keep from messing up, you have to keep growing up. People who are strong in every situation, who inspire people to follow their examples, are learners. Learners are leaders, and leaders learn. When you stop learning, you stop leading. In fact, I believe that if you don't keep learning, you not only stop being a leader; you're in danger of messing up.

Moses is a great example of a leader who was also a learner. Throughout his life he just kept learning from God, from other people and from situations. This is especially evident in Exodus 18.

This was right after the Israelites' big victory over the Amalekites, so you would think that everything was hunky-dory now; they should have glided right up to Mount Sinai. Instead, they came to a very difficult situation, and Moses was about to mess up big time. But God brought someone into his life to give him advice. And because Moses humbled himself, listened and learned, he avoided messing up. He became a better leader by learning from someone else.

To give you a little background, in the first part of chapter 18, Moses met up with his father-in-law, Jethro, and reunited with his wife and sons, whom he had sent back to Midian while he was freeing the Israelites from Egypt. Moses told them all that had happened—the plagues in Egypt, crossing the Red Sea, the water coming out of the rock and the battle against the Amalekites. Jethro gave praise to God and even offered a sacrifice. The elders of Israel joined in for a big feast to celebrate all that the Lord had done for them (see Exod. 18:1–12).

The next morning, Moses went to work. Jethro decided to tag along and see how things were going—and that was when the trouble arose.

> The next day Moses sat to judge the people, and the people stood around Moses from morning till evening. When Moses' father-in-law saw all that he was doing for the people, he said, "What is this that you are doing for the people? Why do you sit alone, and all the people stand around you from morning till evening?" And Moses said to his father-in-law, "Because the people come to me to inquire of God; when they have a dispute, they come to me and I decide between one person and another, and I make them know the statutes of God and his laws." Moses' father-in-law said to him, "What you are doing is not good. You and the people with you will certainly wear yourselves out, for the thing is too heavy for you.

You are not able to do it alone. Now obey my voice; I will give you advice, and God be with you! You shall represent the people before God and bring their cases to God, and you shall warn them about the statutes and the laws, and make them know the way in which they must walk and what they must do. Moreover, look for able men from all the people, men who fear God, who are trustworthy and hate a bribe, and place such men over the people as chiefs of thousands, of hundreds, of fifties, and of tens. And let them judge the people at all times. Every great matter they shall bring to you, but any small matter they shall decide themselves. So it will be easier for you, and they will bear the burden with you. If you do this, God will direct you, you will be able to endure, and all this people also will go to their place in peace."

So Moses listened to the voice of his father-in-law and did all that he had said. (Exod. 18:13–24)

This passage contains specific principles that Moses needed to learn and that you and I can incorporate into our lives so that we can become like those strong people I talked about earlier—lifelong learners who don't mess up their lives because they humble themselves.

UNDERSTAND YOUR PRIORITIES

The first principle that Moses learned from his father-in-law is that we can keep growing by understanding our priorities in life. When Jethro saw Moses presiding over legal disputes, he asked, "Why do you sit alone . . . ?" Then he added, "The thing is too heavy for you. You are not able to do it alone" (Exod. 18:14, 18). The key word here is alone. Jethro had identified a blind spot in Moses' life. Moses was trying to do it all himself, and he thought the answer was to just work harder. But his father-in-law showed him that the answer was to work smarter.

Moses needed someone in his life to help him see his blind spot. God sent Jethro, an older and wiser man, to give him instruction and help him see what he needed to change. Everyone needs people like this—someone who can point out our mistakes and blind spots. They may not always be that tactful, but they are crucial to our success, and God provides them for every one of His followers. But unless you are open to their advice—humble enough to listen and learn—there is a good chance you are going to mess up. One can only imagine how Moses might have messed up if he had not listened to Jethro's advice!

So what was his advice? "Now obey my voice; I will give you advice, and God be with you! You shall represent the people before God and bring their cases to God" (Exod. 18:19). He was saying that Moses was spending a lot of time doing what he shouldn't be doing and not enough time doing what he should. After all, God didn't speak to the people but to Moses, so Moses should have been meeting with God. That was his first priority, but he was spending all his time judging legal issues.

Jethro was telling him to reevaluate his priorities. When people come into our lives and give us advice, they often speak to that same issue. It may sound pretty negative to us, but we should ask ourselves if maybe God is simply reminding us to major on the majors here and not get too involved in minor issues. In Moses' case there were others who could deal with those things, but he was trying to do it alone. There's that key word again.

Jethro is warning Moses that he is on the verge of burnout: "You and the people with you will certainly wear yourselves out" (18:18). In the book *Lord of the Marketplace*, management consultant Myron Rush says that burnout is an evolving process.

It might take anywhere from 20 years to develop or one year to develop, depending on the individual and the circumstances of his job. Yet one thing is for certain: we are on the road to burnout when we try to manage tasks all by ourselves. [xviii]

That's exactly what Moses was doing, and thousands of years later, this management consultant has confirmed Jethro's diagnosis. "You . . . will certainly wear yourselves out" (Exod. 18:18). Rush, who has counseled many victims of burnout and has gone through it himself, says it has a variety of symptoms and identifies two specific ones.

First, people experiencing burnout are very irritable. A burnout victim's nerves are on edge. The smallest incident can touch off a giant emotional explosion. It happened with Moses, and it happened with Jeremiah later in the Bible. They greatly overreact when confronted with problems or difficult situations. Have you seen that in your life? Could you be in danger of messing up simply because you are so irritated?

Second, they are emotionally exhausted. Employees suffering from burnout have no emotional energy left. They suddenly are unable to cope with events and situations that they once had taken in stride. I knew a woman who had been an executive secretary for twenty-five years and was very good at what she did, but her job eventually lost its challenge and she began to experience burnout. One day I walked into her office and found her crying because she had misplaced a roll of tape. To someone experiencing burnout, the most insignificant thing can touch off a crisis with which he or she cannot cope.

I have been on the verge of burnout a few times. Thank God for my coworkers in ministry, lay and clergy, who have come alongside me and been my Jethro, helping me to reevaluate my priorities and see clearly again.

One reason priorities keep changing on us is because life keeps changing. You know how it is: When you're ten or eleven years old, you've really got the kid thing down. Then, boom! The teenage years hit and mess it all up. By the time you've got the teenage thing down, you turn twenty, and all of a sudden you are supposed to be grown up and responsible. Life keeps going through stages like that in your twenties, thirties, forties and so on. If you don't keep changing, you are going to mess up. You have to keep reevaluating your priorities, rethinking who you are and what you are supposed to be doing.

If you are truly seeking to follow God, He will bring others into your life to help you do the reevaluation. Whether it's a small-group Bible study, a Sunday school class or simply one or more individuals in your fellowship, it is very important that you get close to someone. "Iron sharpens iron, and one man sharpens another" (Prov. 27:17). You can hear God speak through someone else helping you. You can't do it alone.

What Jethro is saying to Moses is, "Good grief, open up your life a little! You are trying to do everything yourself." Would God say the same thing to you? The Christian life was never designed for solo operation—just you and your Bible. Those who try to do the "Lone Ranger" routine can't survive. Moses couldn't, and neither can you.

UNDERSTAND YOUR TEACHING

The second point is similar to the first: To keep growing we need to understand our teaching in life. It may sound a little peculiar to put it that way, but what I mean is that all of us teach by our lives. Others learn from you, whether you know you are teaching them or not. Whether it's through your words or your silence, your actions or your inaction, they learn. So it's very important that your life communicates the truth.

For good or for bad, you are a teacher by your life. That's why Jethro's words to Moses apply to all of us: "Twarn them about the statutes and the laws, and make them know the way in which they must walk and what they must do" (Exod. 18:20). What's Jethro's intent? It's pretty clear from the advice he gives later that he wants Moses to reproduce himself: "Look for able men. . . . And let them judge the people " (18:21–22). Reproduce yourself in someone else. This is essential to keep from having to do it all alone.

A friend of mine who grew up in a tough urban neighborhood once made a statement during a Bible study that I will never forget, because he said it with such conviction: "If people aren't taught they become like animals." A similar warning is being issued by Jethro to Moses, only it's the other side of the coin: "Moses, for goodness' sake, teach the people. They are not just a bunch of animals. They can learn to take on responsibility if you teach them."

This means getting involved in someone else's life. Maybe you need to let someone teach you; maybe you need to take what you have learned and be a Jethro for someone else and teach him. We can get so involved in life and its problems that, just like Moses, we forget that this is what it means to live the Christian life. This is how we obey the command of Christ to "go therefore and make disciples . . . teaching them to observe all that I have commanded you" (Matt. 28:19–20).

You may be thinking, I don't know all that much. You might be surprised to discover how much you know that you could pass on to someone else, whether it's through a small group or a one-on-one relationship. You could be very valuable to someone's spiritual walk.

Author Chip MacGregor tells a story in this vein about Sherwood Anderson, author of the widely praised novel *Winesburg Ohio*, who was known for his willingness to help younger writers. In 1919, a soldier recovering from injuries suffered in the great war in Europe asked for Anderson's advice. The two men became fast friends and spent nearly every day together for two years, sharing meals, taking long walks and discussing the craft of writing late into the night.

Anderson was brutally honest in his criticism of the young man's work. The novice took careful notes and then returned to his typewriter to improve his material. Anderson also introduced his young protégé to his network of associates in publishing. In 1926 the young man published his first novel, which met with critical acclaim. Its title was *The Sun Also Rises*, and the author's name was Ernest Hemingway.

But the story does not end there. Anderson moved to New Orleans and met another young wordsmith—a poet with an insatiable drive to improve his skills. Anderson critiqued his work, encouraged him and helped him publish his first novel. Three years later, this bright young talent—William Faulkner—produced *The Sound and the Fury*, which quickly became an American masterpiece.

Anderson's role as a mentor to aspiring authors didn't stop there. In California he spent several years working with Thomas Wolfe and John Steinbeck, among others. All told, three of Anderson's protégés earned Nobel Prizes, and four won Pulitzer Prizes for literature. The famous literary critic Malcolm Coley said that Anderson was the only writer of his generation to leave his mark on the style and vision of the next generation.

The principle that comes out of Anderson's life is that the greatest means of impacting the future is to build into another person's life. Whose life are you building into? I believe that much of the weakness in the North American church is because we've forgotten what discipleship is about. We've forgotten that we are here to reproduce.

What Moses received from God was never meant just for him, and what you receive from God is not just for you. It's given to you to pass on to others. Invest in someone else and your power to change the future will be incredible.

UNDERSTAND YOUR RESPONSIBILITIES

A third point is this: To keep growing, we need to understand our responsibilities in life. We can see this in the advice Jethro gives to Moses. What he is talking about here is learning how to delegate. There is a misconception, however, about delegation—one that I have been guilty of myself—which is that it is simply off-loading work onto other people. That is a very immature understanding of delegation. It is not so much about off-loading work as it is about investing in others—seeing their potential and helping them develop it.

You and I can avoid all kinds of mess-ups in our lives, whether it be with those in our families, at work or in the church, if we look at them as people with great potential whom we can help to develop. That's what Moses needed to see.

John Maxwell, in the book *The 21 Irrefutable Laws of Leadership*, makes an observation about John Wooden, the famous basketball coach, which has a lot to do with delegation. Wooden didn't coach like most coaches. He never scouted opposing teams and he didn't look at the tapes of his opponents to try to analyze their weaknesses.

> Instead he focused on getting his players to reach their potential and he addressed those things through practice and personal interaction with his players. It never was his goal to win championships or even to beat the other team. His desire was to teach each person to play to his potential and to put the best possible team on the floor. And of course Wooden's results were incredible. [xix]

Sports history records that John Wooden had only one losing season in forty years—his first one. He led his UCLA team to four undefeated seasons. That's amazing, and no other coach has ever come close to that record or many of the others that Coach Wooden set. Why? Because they didn't know the vital element of Wooden's approach: To lead means to be excited about others' potential, not your own.

Can you see yourself as a coach, helping someone develop their potential? If you are just off-loading work, you won't get many takers, but if you are excited about developing their potential they will gladly share their hearts with you.

A proverb comes to my mind at this point: "He who separates himself seeks his own desire, He quarrels against all sound wisdom" (Prov. 18:1, NASB). This is what might be called an independent spirit. It is against all sound wisdom to try to do it yourself, to separate yourself and seek your own desire.

Why don't you start praying, *Lord, I need a Jethro. Who is my Jethro?* And maybe you need to be a Jethro to others, passing on what you have learned, teaching them and helping them take responsibility.

Chapter 19

CHOSEN TO BE SOMEBODY

What is the ultimate purpose and meaning of life? Let's hear the thoughts of a few well-known thinkers on this subject:

"The world is all there is and our existence is all we have. You are your life and that's all you are. There is no higher purpose or goal or meaning to life."

—French philosopher Jean-Paul Sartre [xx]

"According to current predictions, the universe is headed for a fiery death and will take us all with it. Nothing we do will outlast our temporary span on this globe. Life is meaningless, purposeless and pointless."

—Nobel Prize-winning physicist Steven Weinberg [xxi]

"Mankind's very existence is an accident, his story a brief and transitory episode in the life of one of the meanest of all planets."

—British philosopher Lord Balford [xxii]

"Man is a product of causes which had no provision of the end they were achieving. His origin, his growth, his hopes and fears, his loves and his beliefs are but the outcome of an accidental collision of atoms."

—British philosopher Bertrand Russell [xxiii]

These guys are pretty depressing, aren't they? Of course, I can quote to you other scientists and philosophers who would strongly disagree with the above conclusions, but I selected these particular men to show what a worldview is like if you leave God out. Without a Creator, you soon come to the same conclusion as these great thinkers did: that life is meaningless, purposeless and futile. You are nothing; your life means nothing; no matter what you have accomplished, you're nobody.

On the other hand, the Bible teaches quite clearly, especially in the story of Moses, that there is a God and an ultimate purpose for mankind—an ultimate meaning to your life. You're not just the result of random chance. In fact, as a follower of God, you are chosen to be somebody—not just in your own mind or in the eyes of this world, but in God's mind, in God's eyes.

The whole premise of the Bible changes your worldview. It helps you to see more accurately how the world really is. It helps you see it from God's point of view, as God's world. When you have a worldview that leaves God out, life is meaningless, stupid, pointless and futile. But if you are a follower of God, you have purpose and meaning in Him and His Word.

This is the reason God gave Israel the Ten Commandments —to show them that in His economy, His plan, His perspective of the world, they had meaning and purpose. It is the same today: From God's perspective, you are somebody. He's calling you to have a purpose and a meaning in your life. When you grab on to these challenges that God places before us in the Old Testament, you gain that meaning and purpose. Let's take a look at some of these challenges in chapters 19 to 34 of Exodus.

CHOSEN TO BE HOLY

The Israelites, after being in the wilderness for several weeks, finally reached Mount Sinai. Back in Exodus 3, God had said He would meet them there after they left Egypt. All the people stayed down in the valley, and Moses went up the mountain. Here's what happened next:

> Moses went up to God. The LORD called to him out of the mountain, saying, "Thus you shall say to the house of Jacob, and tell the people of Israel: You yourselves have seen what I did to the Egyptians, and how I bore you on eagles' wings and brought you to myself. Now therefore, if you will indeed obey my voice and keep my covenant, you shall be my treasured possession among all peoples, for all the earth is mine; and you shall be to me a kingdom of priests and a holy nation. These are the words that you shall speak to the people of Israel." (Exod. 19:3–6)

The first challenge God had for them was to be somebody holy—a holy nation, a chosen people, His prized possession. Moses came down from the mountain and told the people to prepare themselves to meet God. As they stood at the base of the mountain, it must have been pretty exciting: The earth shook; there was lightning, thunder, smoke and the sound of a trumpet in the air. Then God spoke to Moses and gave him the Ten Commandments:

> I am the LORD your God, who brought you out of the land of Egypt, out of the house of slavery.

> You shall have no other gods before me.

> You shall not make for yourself a carved image, or any likeness of anything that is in heaven above, or that is in the earth beneath, or that is in the water under the earth. . . .

> You shall not take the name of the LORD your God in vain, for the LORD will not hold him guiltless who takes his name in vain.

> Remember the Sabbath day, to keep it holy. . . .

Honor your father and your mother, that your days may be long in the land that the LORD your God is giving you.

You shall not murder.

You shall not commit adultery.

You shall not steal.

You shall not bear false witness against your neighbor.

You shall not covet your neighbor's house; you shall not covet your neighbor's wife, or his male servant, or his female servant, or his ox, or his donkey, or anything that is your neighbor's. (Exod. 20:2–4, 7–8, 12–17)

Notice that the first four are about a vertical relationship with God—what it takes to be a holy nation, a chosen people, to be God's treasured possession. The other six are about our horizontal relationships with each other. Chapters 21 to 31 contain a list of more detailed, specific laws: civil laws, criminal laws, covenant laws, laws about the priesthood and how to approach God. But in Exodus 20, God sets the stage with these Ten Commandments, because they were universal—and still are today. They are the basis of much of our modern legal system.

There is a deeper meaning, however, to the Ten Commandments, as Jesus pointed out. In Matthew 22:36–40, Jesus said that the Ten Commandments, as well as the rest of the law and all the words of the prophets, are summed up in these two commands: "Love the Lord your God with all your heart . . . soul . . . mind" (vertical) and "Love your neighbor as yourself" (horizontal). Jesus was saying that all these commandments are about loving relationships.

But many people—even some Christians—look at the Ten Commandments and say, "I don't get it with all these rules and regulations. It seems so strict." But Jesus told us that it's not about rules or laws; it's about relationships. Moses was on the mountain learning how people can get along with each other and with God. How do you have a relationship? Isn't it by treating the other person right? I have found that people usually get along with each other if they don't steal from each other, or commit adultery, or cheat or lie. I heard about a government building in Philadelphia where they were arguing about whether to hang the Ten Commandments on the wall. I wanted to ask, "Which one don't you agree with?"

The Ten Commandments are just basic common sense of how you get along. If you live a life that violates them, there is no possible way you can have good relationships. If you commit adultery and cheat and lie behind others' backs, you won't have good relationships with anybody. No one is going to trust you.

What are the Ten Commandments but the basic fundamental principles of how to love others by building trust? How do you build trust with God? You don't put any other idols before Him or misuse His name. You honor Him and give Him the respect due Him. How do you build trust with people? You don't try to kill them, or talk behind their backs, or lie to them, or covet their wives or their possessions. This is just basic. Anyone would be a fool to deny that. Basic relationship principles build trust.

To the degree that we trust each other with information about ourselves—our feelings, our attitudes, who we are—to that degree we have a relationship. When you don't trust, you don't have a relationship. If that is true of human relationships, isn't it true, then, with God? Why then should it be surprising that God asks us to trust when we come to Christ? It's all about a relationship. God wants a relationship with you. The Ten Commandments are some of the basic principles of how to do it.

In preparation for receiving the commandments, God

told Moses to have the people wash their clothes (see Exod. 19:10). What did that mean? It was a symbolic act of showing cleanness or purity. If the Ten Commandments are all about relationship, it gives a whole new understanding of what holiness is all about. It is not some abstract virtue that we all hope to have some day. Holiness is the fundamental basis of being close to someone on an intimate, personal level.

Take marriage, for example. Why do they call it holy matrimony? Because the word holy means to separate, to cut off. If I'm going to get married, I am going to separate and cut myself off from all other relationships so I can in a special way be united with this other person.

So when God calls us to be holy, a consecrated people, He's saying, "Separate yourself from other things." It means you are going to have to cut off some other things. He even lists the things in the Ten Commandments. Cut yourself off from lying, murderous thoughts, deception, coveting. You have to be wholly dedicated to Him.

Holiness is an all-or-nothing proposition. God said to Moses, "Consecrate those people; have them wash their clothes and get holy; either come to Me completely, wholeheartedly, or don't even come to Me at all." He wants everything or nothing. Just as a husband or wife would say, "You are either all with me or you are not with me at all," it's the same with God. It's the only way you can be with God.

It's really the only way you are supposed to be in a church with each other. You are to be devoted to one another, completely given to one another, caring for each other, helping each other. The church is supposed to be holy. It's what people who follow Christ are supposed to be in their marriages and with their children. Holiness—it's an all-or-nothing proposition.

When I read about God's command to the Israelites to wash their clothes, I think about what He is saying in that image. If you wash your clothes, you don't put them in the washing machine and just turn on the water a little bit, do you? The clothes have to get completely wet. When you want to take a shower and clean your body, do you turn on just a trickle of water? You want the water all over you, the more the better—scrubbing and everything. That's what holiness is—an all-or-nothing proposition. When we do that, it affects all of our relationships.

That was what my friend Ernie discovered. I first met him in the hospital after he had just had a cancerous tumor removed. I shared the gospel with him, and he shed tears, saying, "This is what I have to do. I might have died. I'm not ready to meet my Maker." So he prayed to receive Christ. After praying, he looked up and said, "Does this mean I'll have to quit smoking?"

I said, "Well, I don't know. It's harder for some people than others. I hope you can."

"I don't mean cigarettes," he said. "I mean dope. I've been smoking dope for twenty years."

That might give you an idea what kind of a guy Ernie was. He had been quite a rascal much of his life—through two or three marriages, and his current marriage was in trouble. He was a salesman, and an extremely good one. He could schmooze anyone and get them to buy something. That's what he had done most of his life—schmoozing customers, his wife and his kids, everyone.

A couple years later, after he had been going to church and had grown in his relationship with God, Ernie started taking on holiness. He started developing trust relationships and began to understand some of the fundamentals that are embodied in the Ten Commandments. One day I found him in the chapel, with tears coming down his face. He said, "Marty, when I came to Christ, I had no idea all these changes would take place in my life."

"What do you mean?" I asked.

"Like my wife," he said. "Our dynamic relationship now is incredible. The healing that's taken place is unbelievable. And my kids. I had a daughter who hadn't talked to me for ten years and she's talking to me again." And he started crying once more.

It should be no shock at all. Relationship healing is what the Ten Commandments are all about and what following God and holiness are all about. Being totally devoted and dedicated—all or nothing—heals relationships and makes them strong.

If you think you can have a good, healthy marriage and violate the Ten Commandments, forget about it; you're fooling yourself. If you think you can have good relationships in the church and violate the Ten Commandments, you're crazy. If you think you can have a relationship with God and violate these basic principles of relationships, you are living in a dream.

The New Testament clearly teaches that we are not under the law. We live by the Spirit, and the Spirit helps us keep the law—it is just as basic as that. Ernie's story was a living example of what it's like when you truly let the Spirit of God have control. And it all started back there on the mountain with Moses. That's what the Ten Commandments are all about.

MEANWHILE, BACK AT THE RANCH ...

But while Moses was up on the mountain learning about relationships, holiness and consecration, down in the valley a whole other thing was taking place:

> When the people saw that Moses delayed to come down from the mountain, the people gathered themselves together to Aaron and said to him, "Up, make us gods who shall go before us. As for this Moses, the man who brought

us up out of the land of Egypt, we do not know what has become of him." So Aaron said to them, "Take off the rings of gold that are in the ears of your wives, your sons, and your daughters, and bring them to me." So all the people took off the rings of gold that were in their ears and brought them to Aaron. And he received the gold from their hand and fashioned it with a graving tool and made a golden calf. And they said, "These are your gods, O Israel, who brought you up out of the land of Egypt!" When Aaron saw this, he built an altar before it. And Aaron made a proclamation and said, "Tomorrow shall be a feast to the LORD." And they rose up early the next day and offered burnt offerings and brought peace offerings. And the people sat down to eat and drink and rose up to play. (Exod. 32:1–6)

The word "play" in Hebrew has strong sexual connotations. It means they were involved in all kinds of lewd behavior. They were going back to the pagan practices they had learned in Egypt. It would be like a believer today going back to drugs, alcohol or prostitution. When Moses came down and saw the golden calf and the big orgy going on, he was so angry that he threw the stone tablets containing the Ten Commandments on the ground. They burst into pieces in front of the idol. Then he called for Aaron.

And Moses said to Aaron, "What did this people do to you that you have brought such a great sin upon them?" And Aaron said, "Let not the anger of my lord burn hot. You know the people, that they are set on evil. For they said to me, 'Make us gods who shall go before us. As for this Moses, the man who brought us up out of the land of Egypt, we do not know what has become of him.' So I said to them, 'Let any who have gold take it off.' So they gave it to me, and I threw it into the fire, and out came this calf." (32:21–24)

"I don't know how it happened," Aaron said. "You know these people; they just get out of control." Give me a break!

Couldn't he come up with a better excuse than that? I have a psychologist friend who calls that the "triangle of blame." You either blame your background, your circumstances or other people. Aaron blames both the people ("You know how prone these people are to evil") and the circumstances ("Then they gave me the gold, and I threw it into the fire and out came this calf!"). If only he'd known Freudian psychology, he could have blamed his background too ("You know, I had an unhappy childhood").

Maybe you've been caught in the triangle of blame too. I know I have. You blame this situation or that person or your past and say, "That's just the way I am. I can't help it." You won't get anywhere with that attitude. Your life will continue to be meaningless and purposeless.

CHALLENGED TO BE FAITHFUL

The second thing we learn here is that God challenges us to be faithful. The Israelites were leading faithless lives, stumbling along, not knowing what to do, seeking to feed their hunger and find some meaning in sexual lewdness and idolatry. You may think it strange that they built idols back then, but you and I have idols today too. Throughout the ages, mankind has always made idols—things they follow and give worth to—and worship is just giving worth. What in your life do you give a lot of worth to and get excited about—maybe even put above God? Your spouse could probably tell you.

No matter what idols anyone has ever built, the god he worships is always the same. For every human being, there are only two possible gods in our lives: either the almighty God or ourselves. The Israelites made the calf just the way they wanted and had it do whatever they wanted it to do. Who was the real god? Themselves.

Many people do that with Christianity. They make it the

way they want it so it serves their real god—themselves. Those are common practices down in the valley. That's where Israel was and where many people are, even today. Dallas Willard, in speaking about adultery, shows how this kind of self-worship plays out in a person's life:

> One of the most telling things about contemporary human beings is that they cannot find a reason for not committing adultery. Yet, intimacy, which is what they seek in adultery, is a spiritual hunger of the human soul and we cannot escape it. [xxiv]

Willard is so right in his observation. As a pastor, I have counseled many people who are longing for closer intimacy and who have tried all kinds of sexual exploits to find it, but they always come up empty. Their stories are often filled with great sorrow and pain and are accompanied by many tears.

We violate the Ten Commandments and we know we shouldn't, but we're seeking to fill this intimacy, this hunger in our souls. Then we say that it's her fault, his fault, my circumstances, my past. "I'm just trying to meet this need." It's a big lie.

When Moses got this phony excuse from Aaron, things were looking pretty bleak. What do you do in a situation like that? You do what Moses did:

> And when Moses saw that the people had broken loose (for Aaron had let them break loose, to the derision of their enemies), then Moses stood in the gate of the camp and said, "Who is on the LORD's side? Come to me." And all the sons of Levi gathered around him. (Exod. 32:25–26)

If your life is meaningless and purposeless, if you are living in the triangle of blame and seeking to just satisfy the needs in your life, you need somebody, just as the Israelites did, to get in your face and say, "Whoever is going to follow the Lord, stand with me." There are times in our lives when we need someone to challenge us to be faithful and to follow God day by day, moment by moment. It's our only hope for any meaning or purpose in life. It's a crucial choice, because as we see, those who refused to take the challenge to stand for the Lord paid for it with their lives (see Exod.32:27–28).

The next thing God said to Moses was a complete shock: "Go up to a land flowing with milk and honey; but I will not go up among you, lest I consume you on the way, for you are a stiff-necked people" (33:3). When the people hear it, they begin to mourn, and Moses decides to make an appeal for his people:

> And [Moses] said to [God], "If your presence will not go with me, do not bring us up from here. For how shall it be known that I have found favor in your sight, I and your people? Is it not in your going with us, so that we are distinct, I and your people, from every other people on the face of the earth?"
>
> And the LORD said to Moses, "This very thing that you have spoken I will do, for you have found favor in my sight, and I know you by name." (33:15–17)

What an incredible answer to prayer! In all of Israel, there is one faithful to God—Moses. And when he cries out to God on behalf of all the people, God says, "OK." What power! This is one of the most powerful passages on prayer in the whole Bible. If just one faithful person cries out to God on behalf of the people in the valley—the pagans—God will be merciful.

In Exodus 34, God tells Moses to make two stone tablets like the first ones, so He can write the Ten Commandments on them again. God tells Moses many other things the people need to be reminded of—and after the golden calf incident, it is no surprise that it includes a call to faithfulness: "For you shall worship no other god, for the LORD, whose name is Jealous, is a jealous God" (34:14).

What did God mean by saying He was a jealous God? He

was again challenging Israel to belong solely to Him. God was saying to them, "Do you want Me to belong to you, so that your life has meaning and purpose? Then it's all or nothing for Me. If you want Me to belong to you, then you need to belong to Me." What an appropriate conclusion.

It reminds me of a minor encounter I had with my father when I was about sixteen or seventeen years old. I was living a life of revelry, much like the people of Israel in the valley. I was chasing after pleasures, which was not the way my parents lived; they were strong believers, holy people, wholly devoted to God. It was a Friday night and I was getting ready to go out and have some fun. As I passed my dad in the living room, he said, "Hey, Mart, just a minute."

"Yeah, what do you want?"

He reached into his wallet and pulled out a ten-dollar bill. (This was back when ten dollars was a lot of money.) He said, "Here's some money for gas and stuff like that."

"What for?" I asked.

"Just 'cause you're my boy."

I'm well over fifty now, but I still remember that incident because it had such a powerful impact on me. I held that ten-dollar bill in my hand, thinking, *Dad has no idea whether I might buy some beer or do whatever with this, yet he's saying, "Just 'cause you're my boy."*

I think God set up that incident to begin calling me back to the night when He made it very clear to me, "If you want Me to belong to you, then you need to belong to Me." I know God was speaking to me through my dad.

Maybe God is speaking to your heart. God has given you more than a ten-dollar bill. He's given you basic principles for having sound, strong relationships. He's given you principles for having a meaningful life. He's given you Himself. He's given you His own Son to die on the cross to pay for your sins. He's given you everything. He's saying, "I'll belong to you if you will belong to Me."

Where are you in your life right now? Have you ever been up on the mountain? Have you ever been in the holy place where you are wholly devoted and committed? God challenges you to follow Him up the mountain.

Or are you still down in the valley? Are you still messing around, trying to find meaning and significance by blaming other people, circumstances or your past? Are you still trying to find some meaning in feeding the lusts and desires of your heart? Let me tell you, it isn't going to work. You'll run and chase all your life but you'll never find it. There is nothing there without God.

Maybe you've come to the place where Moses was, where you're ready to say, "Lord, if Your Presence will be with me, I'll do whatever You want; I'll go wherever You want, as long as I belong to You and You belong to me." I hope you come to that place. It's your only hope of any meaning and purpose. Why don't you tell Him that today?

Chapter 20

Disappointment Destroys Lives

One of the most common of human feelings is disappointment. We've all experienced it: from losing the big game to losing a loved one; from being turned down for a date to never being asked; from being overlooked for a promotion to being fired; from losing your money to losing your health. I read recently that the number-one health problem in America—bigger than cancer, heart disease or AIDS—is depression. And disappointment is at the bottom of depression.

So if you are disappointed, you're not alone. Even in the Bible, great spiritual leaders like Moses, Elisha and others went through periods of great disappointment, and they had to learn how to deal with it.

Most of us, however, don't have a great track record in dealing with disappointment. Great athletes and successful business people have seen their careers collapse from drugs, alcohol, anger, immorality or illegality—and it all starts in their hearts with a sense of disappointment. We think that by taking a drink or having an affair we're going to cure the disappointment, but it never works.

Disappointment destroys lives. It could be destroying your life right now, and if you don't learn how to deal with it, you may be its next victim. Moses and the children of Israel went through a time of great disappointment in Numbers 11. Some of the people were destroyed by it, and Moses was about to be, but he made a right turn.

All of us experience disappointment at times, and if we give in to it, it will destroy us. How do we get away from it? By looking at the experience of Moses, maybe we can see how he got so disappointed and how he overcame it.

Why don't we do a case study? Let's pretend that we're professional counselors in a therapy session with a very depressed, disappointed guy named Moses. How would we gain an insight into his problem in order to help him?

1. IDENTIFY THE CAUSE

Well, first of all, like all good counselors and psychologists, we would stroke our chins or adjust our glasses and then say, "Moses, now tell me, where did this all start? When did you start feeling so disappointed with life?" In other words, we want to identify the root cause, right? What's gotten him so disappointed? Moses would begin to explain by telling us a story:

> And the people complained in the hearing of the LORD about their misfortunes, and when the LORD heard it, his anger was kindled, and the fire of the LORD burned among them and consumed some outlying parts of the camp. Then the people cried out to Moses, and Moses prayed to the LORD, and the fire died down. So the name of that place was called Taberah, because the fire of the LORD burned among them. (Num. 11:1–3)

After listening patiently as any good counselor would, you might ask, "Well, Moses, how did that make you feel?" Right? Isn't that what counselors always say? How do you think Moses would respond? He'd probably say, "This is stressing me out. These people are always complaining, and I feel so responsible. The Lord heard them complaining and He came down and struck them with fire. I cried out to Him and He stopped, but I know a lot of them still don't get it. This is the Lord we're talking about."

Next we would probably ask, "OK, Moses, then what happened?"

"Oh, then it got worse," he would respond.

> Now the rabble that was among them had a strong craving. And the people of Israel also wept again and said, "Oh that we had meat to eat! We remember the fish we ate in Egypt that cost nothing, the cucumbers, the melons, the leeks, the onions, and the garlic. But now our strength is dried up, and there is nothing at all but this manna to look at."
>
> Now the manna was like coriander seed, and its appearance like that of bdellium. The people went about and gathered it and ground it in handmills or beat it in mortars and boiled it in pots and made cakes of it. And the taste of it was like the taste of cakes baked with oil. When the dew fell upon the camp in the night, the manna fell with it.
>
> Moses heard the people weeping throughout their clans, everyone at the door of his tent. And the anger of the LORD blazed hotly, and Moses was displeased. (Num. 11:4–10)

Moses might say, "That's when I first noticed how much it was getting to me. Here we are in a desert, surviving on manna, and these people are complaining about the menu! We should be happy we're alive. Good grief, we're in a desert; what do they want?"

As a counselor you might ask, "Then what happened?" And he would respond, "Well, I lost it. I just let God have it, with both barrels." Here's what Moses said to God:

> Moses said to the LORD, "Why have you dealt ill with your servant? And why have I not found favor in your sight, that you lay the burden of all this people on me? Did I conceive

all this people? Did I give them birth, that you should say to me, 'Carry them in your bosom, as a nurse carries a nursing child,' to the land that you swore to give their fathers? Where am I to get meat to give to all this people? For they weep before me and say, 'Give us meat, that we may eat.' I am not able to carry all this people alone; the burden is too heavy for me. If you will treat me like this, kill me at once, if I find favor in your sight, that I may not see my wretchedness." (Num. 11:11–15)

A good counselor always repeats back to the patient what he said, so you might reply, "I hear you saying that you want to pull out of the Lord's call on your life. You don't really want to follow God's plan anymore. Am I hearing you right?"

Moses shifts in his seat and replies, "Well, yeah, that's how I feel. I mean if that's how it's gonna go in this game with me trying to lead these people, I just can't take it anymore." This great leader is disappointed with how life is going, even though he's in the center of God's will.

What's your diagnosis? What's the cause of his depression? Is it the people and their bad attitudes? Maybe if Moses just got away from the people, he'd be fine. That seems to be what Moses is suggesting, and it's not a bad idea. That could be one possibility. Or maybe the problem is with Moses. Counselors often tell their patients to look inward to their own hearts and minds. Maybe you'd tell him, "Moses, you're just being overly responsible—trying to take too much on yourself." Maybe that's part of the problem.

Or is it just the situation? After all, they're in a desert—they're hot, tired and hungry. Maybe all you need to tell Moses is, "Hey, you're feeling a lot of pressure right now. Just calm down and everything will be OK. The people are hungry and tired, so they're a bit cranky. Give them a break, Moses, they'll be all right."

Or is the problem God? Maybe God is the root cause

here. Moses seems to think so. He's blaming God—yelling, accusing, complaining.

Do we get any clue in the text as to the cause of Moses' great disappointment? I think it jumps right off the page. In Numbers 11:11–15, we see personal pronouns repeated over and over again: "Why have I not found favor . . . you lay the burden . . . on me? Did I conceive all this people? Did I give them birth, that you should say to me, 'Carry them in your bosom' . . . ? Where am I to get meat to give to all this people? For they weep before me . . . I am not able to carry all this people alone," and so on.

His focus is on himself: "This violates my rights; it doesn't meet my expectations; this is not my dream for a good life." At the bottom of everyone's disappointment is the same thing. It's as common as dirt. It's why people cheat on their spouses, fall into alcoholism or drugs and lash out in anger. It results from a focus on my point of view, my rights, my expectations.

And anyone who seriously wants to follow God is going to run into this sometime, somewhere, somehow. Moses is just an example of every person who has ever followed God. We all come to a point of decision where it is either God's way or our own way, and we have a choice to make. Are we going to follow disappointment or follow God? Will it be God's plan or our own plans? Are your rights and expectations more important? Jesus addressed this issue when He said, "If anyone would come after me, let him deny himself and take up his cross and follow me" (Matt. 16:24). To truly know God, there is always a step of self-denial.

A pastor friend of mine had a growing church in which he had to deal with all kinds of difficult situations. It became so stressful that he had a heart attack. He went into the hospital to be checked out, and the doctors gave him the OK to go home. A while later, just a week before he was to go on vacation, he started having chest pains again. He went back into the hospital overnight and they checked him all out. Everything looked fine. But just to make sure, they asked him to get on the treadmill before he left the hospital.

He got on the treadmill, and all of a sudden—wham! He started having another heart attack! The next thing he knew, he was going into emergency bypass surgery. "I was mad," he told me later. "I didn't want to do this. I wanted to go on vacation with my family. I was really questioning the Lord." He was just where Moses was. And I'm sure you've been there before too. Something unexpected happens and you say, "No! It wasn't supposed to happen like this!"

So how did it work out with my friend? "It wasn't until I was recovering from surgery a couple of days later that I began to work it through with the Lord," he told me. "Maybe my physical heart was now better, but my spiritual heart was really in bad shape. And me and the Lord had an issue to deal with. It was all about His plan for my life or my plan for my life, His expectations or my expectations."

2. SEEK GOD FOR HELP

It is sad to say, but churches are full of people who come every Sunday who are not fully following the Lord anymore. They are following disappointment, like Moses. If that's where you are, take heart; it's not over yet. The next step after you identify the cause is to seek God's help with your disappointment. That's what Moses did. Even though he didn't have a good attitude, at least he sought the Lord.

Just like Moses, we may react by saying, "I want out." But the game's not over yet. It's like the old phrase, "Please be patient; God is not finished with me yet." That's what Moses needed to remember. It's what my friend with the heart attack finally remembered, and he decided, "OK, Lord, we're following Your plan."

God had an answer for Moses and heard his cry, even in his bad attitude:

> Then the LORD said to Moses, "Gather for me seventy men of the elders of Israel, whom you know to be the elders of the people and officers over them, and bring them to the tent of meeting, and let them take their stand there with you. And I will come down and talk with you there. And I will take some of the Spirit that is on you and put it on them, and they shall bear the burden of the people with you, so that you may not bear it yourself alone. And say to the people, 'Consecrate yourselves for tomorrow, and you shall eat meat, for you have wept in the hearing of the LORD, saying, "Who will give us meat to eat? For it was better for us in Egypt." Therefore the LORD will give you meat, and you shall eat. You shall not eat just one day, or two days, or five days, or ten days, or twenty days, but a whole month, until it comes out at your nostrils and becomes loathsome to you, because you have rejected the LORD who is among you and have wept before him, saying, "Why did we come out of Egypt?"'" (Num. 11:16–20)

Notice that word rejected. When you follow disappointment you reject the Lord. But as for Moses, look at his response:

> But Moses said, "The people among whom I am number six hundred thousand on foot, and you have said, 'I will give them meat, that they may eat a whole month!' Shall flocks and herds be slaughtered for them, and be enough for them? Or shall all the fish of the sea be gathered together for them, and be enough for them?" (11:21–22)

Even though the Lord came up with an answer—He recruited seventy elders to give Moses some help and promised to provide meat for the people to eat—Moses said, "Oh, yeah, right. You can't make them happy." If you've ever done any counseling or tried to help somebody, I'm sure you've heard this statement before. "Oh, you can't make them happy." I've heard people say that about their spouses, their employers, their employees and their kids.

Remember, we're trying to be a counselor for Moses. How would a good counselor respond to that statement? Here's the answer the Lord had for Moses: "Is the Lord's hand shortened? Now you shall see whether my word will come true for you or not" (Num. 11:23).

I've seen a lot of people hurt themselves and other people because they acted like God's arm was too short. They may be very good and faithful people, like Moses. But in one particular emotional dilemma, marriage problem or financial difficulty, they acted as though the Lord's arm was too short. As a result, they turned to cheating on their taxes, lying, having an affair, taking drugs, or something else really wrong, really out there, really wild.

They were feeling so desperate that they let the disappointment push them to the place where they did something that, even in their own judgment, was really hurtful and wrong. There is great power in disappointment. It can drive you to desperation. And at the bottom of it all is a belief that God's arm is just too short, and you say to yourself, "I'm going to take care of this on my own." Boy, you're on dangerous ground then!

Counseling Moses is getting pretty complex; we don't quite know what to do with him. Let's ask another psychiatrist for help. Dr. Frank Minirth taught a class I attended, in which he told us that he used to have depression himself. He said he even had a personality type that tends to lean toward depression. As he explained that, many of us realized we were just like him.

Then he went on to share with us the secret that helped him out of depression. He said it was based around the idea of being able to hear from God. You and I could look at Numbers 11 and say, "Moses was lucky; God would just talk to him. I'd sure like it if He talked with me." Dr. Minirth would say,

"Well, you can hear from God."

This is good news, because there are times, especially times of great disappointment, when you need to hear a word from the Lord. That's why you're so depressed and disappointed—you want to hear from the Lord. You need some assurance and help. So, what do you do?

In response to that question, Dr. Minirth pulled out of his pocket a set of cards. He said, "On these three-by-five cards I have verses from the Bible. And I use these to encourage myself, to build myself up. This is the medication that I prescribe for depression. It works great for me." The key to avoiding disappointment, he told us, is to hear from the Lord through memorizing Scripture.

When he said that, I thought, *Here's a guy with a medical degree, a psychiatrist, whose profession is helping people with severe difficulties, and he says the best prescription you can get is Bible verses?* He said, "It works for me." It worked for me too, and I've seen it work for others. Isn't that what happened in Numbers 11? Moses was so down, he said, "I have to hear from the Lord." And he did.

You and I can still hear from the Lord. The answers are there in the Holy Scriptures. It's up to us to use them. Writing verses out on three-by-five cards, reading the Bible privately, going to a Bible study—whatever it takes—is a real key. I honestly don't know how any follower of God could avoid disappointment without constantly hearing from God. The only way Moses could get out of his depression was to hear a fresh word from the Lord. And there comes a point in our lives when, maybe even on a daily basis, you need to hear from the Lord. I encourage you to do that.

A man in my church put this into practice when his eighteen-year-old daughter died. The worst thing any parent can imagine is to see his child in a casket. After the funeral, he went away on vacation with his three other kids. "On vacation I had a challenge for each of my children," he told me. "Whenever we gathered together for family time, they had to share a Bible verse or a Scripture passage they were hanging on to—a promise from God."

People look at this family in our church that has suffered such a tragedy, and they wonder how they are doing so well. How are they getting through this crisis? They're hearing from the Lord. This is just what you and I need to do—especially through crises, through times of great disappointment. We desperately need to hear from the Lord, and His Word is where we hear His voice. We need to hang on to it for all we are worth. That's what Moses needed to do.

3. CHOOSE THE CALL OF GOD

It all comes down to a decision. You need to choose the call of God over the call of disappointment. And disappointment calls to you and me, saying, "Hey, you need more money; you need more respect; you need more sensual pleasure." And you find yourself thinking, *How come others get to do this or that when I don't? Why does that person have so much when I have so little? Why do I have to be single, or divorced, or unemployed, or sick? Why do all these terrible things happen to me?*

Disappointment calls to your heart all the time. And you can see in Scripture that there's a mastermind behind this god of disappointment—the devil himself. He's crying out to your heart all the time: "Hey, you need more; you should get more." And you will either decide to follow disappointment or follow the Lord. It's one or the other; you can't do both. And what God does to Israel next points that out graphically:

> Then a wind from the Lord sprang up, and it brought quail from the sea and let them fall beside the camp, about a day's journey on this side and a day's journey on the other side, around the camp, and about two cubits above the

ground. And the people rose all that day and all night and all the next day, and gathered the quail. Those who gathered least gathered ten homers. And they spread them out for themselves all around the camp. While the meat was yet between their teeth, before it was consumed, the anger of the LORD was kindled against the people, and the LORD struck down the people with a very great plague. Therefore the name of that place was called Kibroth-hattaavah, because there they buried the people who had the craving. (Num. 11:31–34)

The Lord judged the people who had rejected Him and were following disappointment. Here we have the clear idea that when you follow disappointment it destroys your life. It's a graphic illustration of what we need to see about disappointment: When you hear its call and follow it, you're taking the path of your own destruction and of the destruction of your loved ones around you as well. But when you turn from disappointment and say, "I'm gonna follow the Lord," that is called faith. In light of the great disappointments in life, you decide by faith to follow the Lord anyway. Job had it right when he said, "Though he slay me, I will hope in him" (Job 13:15).

I have had three major disappointments in my life where I had to decide to either hear the call of disappointment or hear the call of God. When I was growing up, I had one major disappointment: I couldn't read. I have dyslexia. It was very embarrassing and may have had a lot to do with why I was so rebellious. I was angry and I lashed out.

When I was eighteen, I heard God's call and turned to Christ. And by turning to Christ, I decided to turn away from disappointment and anger and bitterness and lashing out. I decided to follow the Lord. And guess what? He taught me how to read. And all of a sudden I learned it; I read so well, I went to college, then seminary, graduating with an A average.

That grade was impossible for a guy like me, but it happened. Why? Because I didn't follow the god of disappointment anymore, but the God of miracles, the God who changes people's lives.

My next great disappointment came after I moved across the country and started a church. I got a phone call that my father was sick. Two days later I was told he was dead. I didn't get to say good-bye. I was very disappointed. I told the Lord, "My dad and I were just starting to relate man-to-man, and now you take him home? What's with this?" I had to decide between following disappointment and getting depressed or holding onto God's Word and following Him.

Then I got sick in 1992 with the Epstein-Barr virus and didn't work for nine months. I was very disappointed. "Lord, why do I have to have this sickness? Why does this have to happen to me?" I was hearing the call of disappointment loud and clear. But I had another choice.

And you know what? I'm probably not done yet. God is not finished with me yet; He's not finished with you. But He takes us along the way in steps and stages. And at each step I have to decide again, am I going to follow disappointment or am I going to follow the Lord? How deep is my faith? How much do I believe in God's everlasting love and care for me? And if I've truly surrendered to His plan, can I follow it, even when what I expected didn't happen, even when dreams didn't come true? I have to make a choice.

If we were in a counseling session with Moses, we would have to remember another thing that counselors always tell us: Change cannot happen unless the patient really wants to change. That's really true. The counselor can only lead us to the point where we finally say, "OK, I understand the problem. The Lord has been speaking to my heart. Now what?" Now you need to make a choice.

Chapter 21

Dealing with Unjust Criticism

I read a story about a wealthy man who decided to move from Colorado to Texas. In the plains of West Texas, he built a mansion with a huge picture window overlooking the prairie. He said, "I love to sit and look out my picture window. The problem is, there's nothing to see!" About the same time, another wealthy man moved from West Texas to Colorado and built a mansion on the side of a mountain. He said, "I love my house in Colorado. The problem is, when I look out my picture window, I can't see anything because the mountain is in the way!"

It's amazing how we can look at something beautiful and totally miss what's going on—we become critical. All of us have participated in criticism, even unjust criticism. If we analyze ourselves, we might even find that we do it daily. Some families have it down to a fine art!

I'm sure all of us have been on the receiving end of unjust criticism as well, whether from our parents or some other relative, our spouse, a friend, a coworker or somebody at church. We felt unjustly criticized, and it hurt deeply.

I think most everyone knows the destructive, hurtful, debilitating and anger-producing effects of criticism. There are people who have had the whole direction of their lives changed by unjust criticism. Because of criticism, people have changed jobs, changed neighborhoods, changed spouses, changed the church they go to, changed all kinds of things. We work hard to be "nice," so no one ever does it to us again. We have learned coping mechanisms to deal with criticism, but I'm not sure that's the right way.

Throughout the Bible, one character quality is identified over and over again as the way to deal with criticism, especially unjust criticism: humility. Jesus said, "Whoever humbles himself like this child is the greatest in the kingdom of heaven" (Matt. 18:4). In the midst of criticism—or any kind of life experience, for that matter—you need to exemplify humility to be honored in God's kingdom. In another passage Jesus said, "Whoever exalts himself will be humbled, and whoever humbles himself will be exalted" (23:12). Criticism often involves someone putting you down. Jesus says to respond with humility and God will exalt you.

The question is, what does humility in response to criticism look like? Does it always mean being quiet? Are you supposed to be some kind of doormat? Numbers 12 gives us the great advantage of seeing it lived out by one of the most humble men recorded in Scripture—Moses.

Let's imagine somebody just criticized you—I mean, you were ridiculed, mocked and harshly, unjustly criticized. And you are crushed. So you go home with your chin dragging. You walk in the door and there is a tall, gray-haired, grandfatherly old man named Moses who says, "You just got criticized."

You look at him and say, "How did you know?"

He says, "Well, I know the look. I've been there before. If you have a few minutes before you go upstairs and cry on your pillow, sit down and we'll talk about it." Isn't it great when an old guy takes you under his wing and teaches you a few things? And one thing we've learned about Moses is that he knew how to deal with criticism. He had a lot of practice. So he sits you down and says, "In my long career I've learned a few things about criticism. I'd like to tell you about three instances when I was harshly, unjustly criticized and how I dealt with it."

KEEPING SILENT BEFORE YOUR CRITICS

He begins with one of the toughest experiences he ever had to deal with: "Everything was going fine; we had been through a lot of tough stuff, but the future was looking bright. That's why I felt totally blindsided when my own brother, Aaron, and my own sister, Miriam, started saying I was getting too big for my britches. 'You're not the only one who hears from the Lord,' they told me. 'Who do you think you are, setting yourself up as the big boss around here?' I was shocked. I couldn't believe that my own family members would criticize me.

"They were also upset with my choice of a wife. Miriam never did get along with her, and Aaron didn't like her very much, either. That was part of the complaint."

Of course, you can sense what he's feeling, so you ask, "Mr. Moses, what did you do?"

"Well, I didn't know what to do. I was so taken aback that I just prayed to the Lord, and I felt the Lord giving me strength in my heart. I decided not to say a word. There was nothing I could say anyway. My brother and sister had been with me from the beginning. They should have known what my life was all about. Besides, the Lord comforted my heart in the midst of it.

"I was silent, but the Lord wasn't. He said, 'I want all three of you to go to the Tent of Meeting outside the camp.' When we got out to the Tent of Meeting, this big cloud came over the meeting place, and the Lord pulled Miriam and Aaron aside and said, 'When I speak to prophets, I speak to them in dreams, and I speak to them in visions like I have spoken to you. But when I speak to my servant Moses, I speak to him outright, without any riddles—straight out, because he is My friend. How dare you speak to My friend Moses like you did!'

"All of a sudden the cloud was gone. We looked around and there was Miriam and her flesh was all flaky and white. She had leprosy. She started screaming, thinking she was going to die a long, agonizing death. Aaron turned to me and said, 'Moses, you can't let this happen to Miriam. Cry out to God.' So I fell on my knees and I cried out, 'Dear God, please heal Miriam. Be merciful to her.' And God said to us, 'I'll heal her, but just like a child who needs to be disciplined, I want you to send her outside the camp for seven days. There are consequences that she has to face.' So Miriam was sent out of the camp for seven days. When she came back, all the leprosy was gone; she was healed" (see Num. 12:1–15).

You might ask, "Mr. Moses, what did all that mean?" He would reply, "I learned that sometimes the right response to criticism is to be silent and let the Lord do the talking for you."

I'm sure that Moses would also point out this recurring theme he has seen: Weak leaders often criticize others to try to put themselves above them. There is a glaring contrast between Miriam and Aaron's arrogance and Moses' humility. That's what God wants us to learn in this story—the difference between a true leader's humility and a "wannabe" leader's arrogance. When you are arrogant and critical, you are just a "wannabe" leader, and you are going to be put down. But when you humble yourself you become a true leader.

Notice that Moses' silence is also in contrast to our normal responses. Usually when we are criticized, we try to explain ourselves, or our anger flares up, or we plan a counterattack. I've done that and I'm sure you have too. You want to say, "No, that's not true; let me explain," or justify your actions, or argue back, or defend yourself—maybe even attack them back.

Why, then, was Moses so silent? The reason is alluded to in the text, as well as in Moses' whole life. As a man who is close to the Lord, Moses' heart was quiet so his mouth was quiet. A person speaks out of his mouth what's down in his heart (see Matt. 12:34). If your heart is quiet, your mouth will be quiet. You'll have a real hard time keeping your mouth quiet if your heart is not. Moses is quiet because his heart is with the Lord. His strength is in the Lord. And because he has a quiet heart, he is humble. The text tells us he was the most humble man on the face of the earth (see Num. 12:3). To endure in the midst of an outpouring of criticism against you or those you love requires humility, a humility that can be silent just as Christ was when He was under attack.

The only way we can be silent when we are criticized unjustly is to be close to the Lord. If you have your shelter, your strength, your stronghold in the Lord, no criticism can shake you. You are at peace because you are so tight with the Lord. That's your only hope. That's how Moses pulled this off. He was truly humble, and humility is quietness in your heart, which only comes from the Lord.

Years ago, someone said something about me that was very unjust and critical—and I definitely did not have a quiet heart about it. I was very upset and had the normal response to it: I started making a battle plan. I was figuring out a counterattack; I was going to explain myself. That's when an elder in my church, my senior by a few years, pulled me aside and said, "Marty, calm down."

I said, "What do you mean?" He replied, "It's going to be OK. The Lord is still on the throne, and He's going to deal with this." He did exactly the right thing. He pointed me to the Lord. That's the answer every time. What does the Lord think? Can the Lord deal with this? Moses was silent, and the Lord spoke. Be silent. Sometimes the greatest power you can have is to say nothing, to do nothing to explain yourself or defend yourself.

CHALLENGING YOUR CRITICS

As you are listening to Moses explain all these things, you would probably ask, "But are you always supposed to be quiet? Aren't you ever supposed to say anything?" And Moses would say, "Well, as a matter of fact, no, you're not supposed to always be quiet. Sometimes you are supposed to speak. Let me tell you another story.

"It was some time after that occurrence when three Israelite leaders—Korah, Dathan and Abiram—came to meet with me. I had heard rumblings in the camp that these guys were not pleased with how things were going. They didn't like the directions we were taking or some of the decisions I had been making. So they started to criticize me.

"One day they showed up with 250 other leaders and council members, and said, 'Moses, we believe you have gone too far. You hold yourself up as some kind of holy man, but we are all holy in God's eyes. God speaks through us and leads through us too. You act like you are the only one in charge. We want more decision-making power. We think we could do a better job if we got involved with you'" (see Num. 16:1–3).

What did Moses do? "Well, I did what I always do," he said. "I fell on my face before God and I began to pray. But this time as I prayed, God did not let my heart be silent. God agitated me and showed me that I needed to speak— to challenge them. So I rose to my feet and said, 'The big question is, What does God want?'"

When you have a critic in your face, sometimes you need to remind him—and yourself—of that point: What does God want? Korah, Dathan and Abiram said that God wanted them and the other leaders to be more involved in making decisions; Moses said that God had been leading them rightly. So Moses challenged them to go out to the Tent of Meeting and let God sort it out. Here's how it happened.

And Moses said, "Hereby you shall know that the LORD has sent me to do all these works, and that it has not been of my own accord. If these men die as all men die, or if they are visited by the fate of all mankind, then the LORD has not sent me. But if the LORD creates something new, and the ground opens its mouth and swallows them up with all that belongs to them, and they go down alive into Sheol, then you shall know that these men have despised the LORD."

And as soon as he had finished speaking all these words, the ground under them split apart. And the earth opened its mouth and swallowed them up, with their households and all the people who belonged to Korah and all their goods. So they and all that belonged to them went down alive into Sheol, and the earth closed over them, and they perished from the midst of the assembly. (Num. 16:28–33)

Here Moses challenges his critics, but previously he had been silent. If Moses was telling you this story, I'm sure your first question would be, "How do I know when to be quiet and when to challenge?" The answer to that question is in two statements Moses made: "The LORD has sent me to do all these works . . . it has not been of my own accord" (16:28) and "then you shall know that these men have despised the LORD" (16:30).

Notice that Moses is not worried about his own ideas or that he himself is being treated with contempt. Moses is defending the Lord's ideas and the Lord's honor. How do you know, from the example of Moses, when to challenge and when to be quiet? You challenge when it's not about you— your ideas or your honor—but about the Lord and His ideas, His honor. That's when it's right to challenge. But if it's about you, keep your mouth shut.

Moses had the right to challenge. Jesus had the right to challenge. The apostle Paul had the right to challenge, and in every case, they challenged when it wasn't about them. That's a very important distinction.

A man who influenced me a lot in the past twenty years

of my life was my father-in-law. He'd been a pastor for thirty-seven years and helped me a lot in understanding what it means to be a pastor. He also became the president of a seminary after that and later president of his denomination. Now he is home with the Lord.

When he was a seminary president, my family and I visited him during a period when a lot of the faculty were criticizing what he was doing. These were highly educated and intelligent men, maybe even more intelligent than he was, saying that he wasn't doing things right. At that same time a group of people was encouraging him to run for president of the denomination. But another group of people was criticizing him for considering it.

Despite all these things happening, he seemed to have such a quiet heart, and I asked him why. He said, "Well, there is a lot of pressure, a lot of criticism, but I'm challenging my critics."

When I asked him about the presidency of the denomination, he just said, "Marty, it's fine with me." You should have seen the peace on his face—his total contentment. People were raking him over the coals, and he was totally peaceful. He said, "I've been a pastor for thirty-seven years. I have nothing more to prove. If it happens, it happens. If it doesn't, I don't care. I'm just following the Lord."

No wonder he could challenge his critics! It wasn't about him. He didn't have to prove to anybody how well he could do it or how tough he was or how strong he was. When it's about your ideas or your honor, you better be careful what you say. But when it's about the Lord and His kingdom and about accomplishing what the Lord has called you to do, that's a whole different story. Now you have something with which to challenge your critics.

I read a book a while ago in which the author defines

humility as self-forgetfulness—not demeaning yourself, not putting yourself down, not thinking less of yourself, but self-forgetfulness. Just as my father-in-law said: "I don't have to impress anybody. I have nothing to prove." He was just forgetting about himself. Moses was just forgetting about himself. It's about forgetting yourself in the Lord.

COMING TO THE AID OF YOUR CRITICS

I understand through Moses that sometimes we are supposed to be silent and sometimes we are supposed to challenge, but isn't there more to it? It seems like it often gets more complicated than that, especially when people persist in attacking or criticizing us. I think Moses would tell us the next story which is also in Numbers 16, beginning with verse 41: "But on the next day all the congregation of the people of Israel grumbled against Moses and against Aaron, saying, 'You have killed the people of the LORD.'"

Can you believe that—the next day? Their friends had just gotten eaten by the earth, but they were gutsy enough—or stupid enough—to continue to criticize. They must have been addicted to grumbling; they couldn't seem to quit. Here's what happened next:

> And when the congregation had assembled against Moses and against Aaron, they turned toward the tent of meeting. And behold, the cloud covered it, and the glory of the LORD appeared. And Moses and Aaron came to the front of the tent of meeting, and the LORD spoke to Moses, saying, "Get away from the midst of this congregation, that I may consume them in a moment." And they fell on their faces. And Moses said to Aaron, "Take your censer, and put fire on it from off the altar and lay incense on it and carry it quickly to the congregation and make atonement for them, for wrath has gone out from the LORD; the plague has begun." So Aaron took it as Moses said and ran into the

midst of the assembly. And behold, the plague had already begun among the people. And he put on the incense and made atonement for the people. And he stood between the dead and the living, and the plague was stopped. Now those who died in the plague were 14,700, besides those who died in the affair of Korah. And Aaron returned to Moses at the entrance of the tent of meeting, when the plague was stopped. (Num. 16:42–50)

I don't know about you, but I read that and I say, "What's going on here?" Doesn't it appear like the Lord is acting immaturely and Moses and Aaron are acting maturely? Doesn't it look like Moses and Aaron are holding it together but the Lord is losing control? That's exactly what God wants you to see. The Lord is practicing the principle I mentioned earlier, that He exalts the humble and puts down the proud.

God is lifting up Moses and Aaron so high that the people have to go to them, because they will be too afraid to go to God. God is actually lowering Himself to raise them up. Isn't that ingenious? That's the Lord. Even if He has to make Himself look bad to exalt Moses and Aaron, He is willing to do it, to make sure the people will follow them.

But this plan of God's would never have worked if Moses and Aaron had not come to the aid of the people. Because they did that, God could exalt them. What a lesson! If you can be humble to the extent that you actually come to the aid of your critics, God can even exalt you in their eyes. After this incident, the people said, "We're following Moses. He knows what he's doing. He saved our lives."

A lot of people never see that power of humility in their lives because they are too busy fighting it—defending themselves, strategizing how to avoid the pain and the problem—instead of saying, "I'm going to help my critics."

I learned this early in my Christian life. Over thirty years ago, when I had just become a Christian and was learning to share my faith, my friend Rob and I used to go to a shopping mall and share the gospel with the kids who were hanging out there. We had literally hundreds of kids praying with us to receive Christ.

An older guy used to show up who was definitely more knowledgeable and smarter than we were. He constantly criticized, mocked and ridiculed us in front of the kids, ruining our whole ministry. He was obviously doing drugs and maybe even selling drugs to the kids. Maybe that was part of why he gave us such a hard time. Every time he saw us coming he'd smile with glee because he had another chance to rip us up. I was just a baby Christian; I didn't know how to defend myself or anything.

At one point, Rob said, "Marty, we just have to stay humble. We have to help this guy. Maybe we can buy him lunch." So we did that one day. We continued to talk with him and tried to listen to his arguments. Nothing seemed to work, however.

A year later Rob and I were at a Christian concert, standing in the lobby jammed like sardines, waiting for the doors to open. About fifteen yards away, I saw that guy from the mall. I thought, *What is he doing here? Oh no—he sees me!* His eyes locked with mine, and he started coming over to me. I didn't know whether to run or stay.

Once he worked his way through the crowd and got over to me, he said, "Hey, great to see you." He hugged me and started weeping. "I just want to thank you for telling me the gospel," he said. "I've become a Christian. You have no idea what an impact you had on me."

God was teaching me, even back then, that if you minister to your critic, the power of God is released. This guy came over and exalted me like I'm some great guy. All I did was try to witness to him. Isn't the power of humility amazing?

If we were listening to Moses tell us these stories, we would probably say, "OK, I think I understand. When I am criticized, sometimes the best response is to be silent because my strength needs to be in the Lord. Sometimes I need to challenge my critics, but only when it's not about me or my honor, but about the Lord's honor. And sometimes I even have to get to a place where I'm humble enough that I'll actually minister to my critic.

"But I have one question, Mr. Moses: Why does the Lord let His servants get so criticized?"

I can just see old Moses sitting there stroking his beard and saying, "Well, son, looking back on my life, I can see that criticism drove me to the Lord—and that was a good thing. It was painful and hard, but I'm afraid that without it I would have just drifted away. Criticism, my son, will either drive you to the Lord or drive you away."

It's true—criticism will either drive you closer to or further away from the Lord. Don't let it drive you away. The power of humility is the answer to criticism. Draw nearer to God, not further away. It's your only hope. It is maturity. It is the way to grow.

In this sinful world, you are going to get criticized. That's life. It might even come from your loved ones. But if your heart is quiet with the Lord, so what? If it's not about you, so what? If you are there to minister, then minister to them, so what? The answer to criticism is humility. That's what Moses would say.

Chapter 22

MAKING AN IMPACT

As I have worked with people over many years I've come to notice a common passion inside all of us: desire to make an impact, to make a difference, to be significant. Whether it's having an impact in our families, the church, the community or the workplace, we all have this desire, this longing. As we've seen recently in the news, some people will literally strap bombs to their bodies and walk into a group of people and blow themselves up to make an impact for their cause. Others will take vows of celibacy and live in monasteries to make an impact for God. Others will take a sport and study it from childhood, spending hours and days, investing their whole lives to make an impact in that sport. All of us have this longing, this passion inside of us to make an impact, to leave our mark, if even on a small scale.

Well, if that is true—and I think it is—then the most instructive person to help us with this would be Moses. Moses made a bigger impact than almost any human being who has ever lived throughout human history. Many nations around the world, including the United States, are structured after the basic understandings of law and social structure as taught by Moses thousands of years ago.

We listen to self-appointed experts on TV infomercials, who offer to teach us how to be significant through their seminars, tapes and self-help books. Which gets me to thinking—what if Moses did a TV show? What if Moses wrote a self-help book? Would he say, "Here are the three principles to significance," or "If you follow these five steps, you will really make an impact on society"? What would he teach?

Whatever he had to say, I would certainly listen. I think anyone would be a fool not to listen to Moses, because all these other self-help people are nothing compared to Moses. Who else has a few-thousand-year track record of making an impact on the human race? Hardly anybody has ever made more of an impact.

I think I know what Moses would teach; toward the end of his life it became very clear what his message would be. There are three particular things I think he would say.

1. AVOID SELF-IMPORTANCE

The first is: Don't be overcome by your own self-importance, but be humble. Numbers 12:3 says, "Now the man Moses was very meek, more than all people who were on the face of the earth." If Moses were doing a seminar or a self-help book, this would be principle number one. He'd probably say something like, "Humility is the key that unlocks the door to significance in your life," or some snazzy statement like that. He would tell you, "It is the key to all of my successes. All those around me were defeated by their own pride and ego. Humility is the key to all my strength."

And he'd probably also say, "The biggest mistake I ever made in my life was when I wasn't humble." And then he'd go on to tell us the story that's recorded in Numbers 20:

> And the people of Israel, the whole congregation, came into the wilderness of Zin in the first month, and the people stayed in Kadesh. And Miriam died there and was buried

there.

Now there was no water for the congregation. And they assembled themselves together against Moses and against Aaron. And the people quarreled with Moses and said, "Would that we had perished when our brothers perished before the LORD! Why have you brought the assembly of the LORD into this wilderness, that we should die here, both we and our cattle? And why have you made us come up out of Egypt to bring us to this evil place? It is no place for grain or figs or vines or pomegranates, and there is no water to drink." (Num. 20:1–5)

Does this sound familiar? We have heard this story before, haven't we? But it's happening again.

Then Moses and Aaron went from the presence of the assembly to the entrance of the tent of meeting and fell on their faces. And the glory of the LORD appeared to them, and the LORD spoke to Moses, saying, "Take the staff, and assemble the congregation, you and Aaron your brother, and tell the rock before their eyes to yield its water. So you shall bring water out of the rock for them and give drink to the congregation and their cattle." And Moses took the staff from before the LORD, as he commanded him.

Then Moses and Aaron gathered the assembly together before the rock, and he said to them, "Hear now, you rebels: shall we bring water for you out of this rock?" And Moses lifted up his hand and struck the rock with his staff twice, and water came out abundantly, and the congregation drank, and their livestock. And the LORD said to Moses and Aaron, "Because you did not believe in me, to uphold me as holy in the eyes of the people of Israel, therefore you shall not bring this assembly into the land that I have given them." These are the waters of Meribah, where the people of Israel quarreled with the LORD, and through them he showed himself holy. (Num. 20:6–13)

Here is a story of Moses violating the basic principle he

lived by—humility. He showed his pride and arrogance. You can see it in his anger, when he calls the people "you rebels." You can also see it very clearly when he says, "Must we bring water out of this rock?"—as if Moses and Aaron, and not the Lord, were going to do it! It is also significant that Moses struck the rock twice, when the Lord told him to speak to the rock.

You might see these as minor offenses, and in some sense they were. But the real problem was his pride. And just like any other human being, pride was the first step to his downfall. The most significant thing he was living for in the latter part of his life was the Promised Land, but God said, "I'm not going to let you walk in." This must have been very discouraging.

Moses would say, "This was my biggest mistake. Pride caused me great pain and great defeat, just as it had my enemies." I could illustrate this with a lot of different people whom we know. There are leaders of business whose ego and pride took over and who hurt many people as a result. And now their downfall has come and their impact is lost.

Or I could mention American presidents, such as Richard Nixon or Bill Clinton. That would be significant and we could learn some lessons. But that's the negative side of it. What if we looked at the positive side? Do we have a record of someone who turned from his ego and pride to humility? The answer is yes.

I read an article a while ago by Stephen King, the author of all those scary novels. I've never read one of his books and I'm not recommending them, but I highly recommend this article, because in it King tells about his turn toward humility. It happened after he was involved in a severe accident. It's called "What You Pass On."

> A couple of years ago, I found out what "You can't take it with you" means. I found out while I was lying in a ditch at the side of a country road covered with mud and

blood. And with the tibia of my right leg poking out the side of my jeans like the branch of a tree taken down in a thunderstorm. I had a MasterCard in my wallet. But when you're lying in a ditch with broken glass in your hair no one accepts MasterCard. [xxv]

King goes on to describe the entirely new feelings that swept over him and how he began to get a new perspective on life. He talked of powerful people, like Warren Buffet, Bill Gates and Tom Hanks, saying that they may have lots of money and fame now, but when they die they won't be able to take a dime with them. King said that his newfound reality counsels him to reevaluate his life and his values. He ends the article with the following advice: "So I want you to consider making your life one long gift to others. And why not? All you have is on loan anyway. All that lasts is what you pass on." [xxvi]

What Stephen King experienced is humility. It's the key that unlocks the door to significance. And he understood that the way to be significant is to give your life away to others. That's true humility. The definition of humility is self-forgetfulness. It's coming to the place where you realize the only thing that really matters is what you pass on to others. What a powerful truth.

It's the same thing Moses would teach in his seminar or write in his book. You want to be significant? You want to make an impact? You want to make a difference with your kids, your church, your community, your world? Realize that you can't take anything with you. The only things that will last are what you give away, what you pass on to others.

I hope you don't have to be lying in a ditch somewhere bleeding to death before you finally get it. We can hear the Scriptures. We can hear wise old Moses speak and can say to ourselves, "That's right, I have to change my tune here." I challenge you to not think so highly of yourself, but to take on humility. That's the first thing Moses would teach us.

2. DON'T BE AFRAID

The second thing he would teach us is: Don't be afraid, but be strong and courageous in the Lord. I know that's exactly what Moses would say, because he did say that. Moses gathered everybody in Israel together to say his good-byes. He passed his ministry on to the children of Israel and had them take it from there on their own.

> So Moses continued to speak these words to all Israel. And he said to them, "I am 120 years old today. I am no longer able to go out and come in. The LORD has said to me, 'You shall not go over this Jordan.' The LORD your God himself will go over before you. He will destroy these nations before you, so that you shall dispossess them, and Joshua will go over at your head, as the LORD has spoken. And the LORD will do to them as he did to Sihon and Og, the kings of the Amorites, and to their land, when he destroyed them. And the LORD will give them over to you, and you shall do to them according to the whole commandment that I have commanded you. Be strong and courageous. Do not fear or be in dread of them, for it is the LORD your God who goes with you. He will not leave you or forsake you."
>
> Then Moses summoned Joshua and said to him in the sight of all Israel, "Be strong and courageous, for you shall go with this people into the land that the LORD has sworn to their fathers to give them, and you shall put them in possession of it. It is the LORD who goes before you. He will be with you; he will not leave you or forsake you. Do not fear or be dismayed." (Deut. 31:1–8)

Try to get a picture of the scene: Here's this 120-year-old guy teaching these people. You can hear it in his words that he's speaking from experience, and he's saying, "Don't be overcome by fear."

What is fear? It is basically self-protection. When God first appeared to Moses, he gave Him every excuse in the book why he couldn't do it. He was afraid. But when he headed into that fear and stopped thinking about protecting himself, that was the key to his success. That was when he became significant and started making a difference. But whenever he started thinking about himself and protecting what he had, that's when he started going wrong and had a very insignificant life. So, don't be overcome by fear. Instead be strong, be courageous, head out.

One of the biggest enemies you and I fight is fear—protecting ourselves with our bank accounts, our investments, our houses, our securities, etc. That's what stops us from being significant, from really making a difference. There are times when you need to fly in the face of your fear, whether it's fear for your health, your sanity or your loved ones. It's a choice you make. Moses did it over and over again, so he's speaking from experience.

I wonder what Joshua must have been feeling. Moses turned to him in front of everybody and said, "Joshua, I'm passing the mantle to you now." Then he told him the same thing he had just told all the people: "Don't be afraid; be strong and courageous. The Lord will never leave you or forsake you." Those promises are still true for you and me.

I'm sure a lot of the people there looked at Moses as their hero. They wanted to be like him. I certainly do, when I read his story, and I hope you do too. As I looked at his life, I began thinking that he's just like some of the heroes God has brought into my life.

One of my first heroes was Maude Johnson, a seventy-five-year-old retired schoolteacher. She lived in a western suburb of Minneapolis, and her husband and son had just died after long illnesses. Maude could have listened to her fears—her need for self-protection. Anybody would have said it was justified for a woman seventy-five years old and living in grief. No one would expect her to think of ministering, of being concerned for others, of making a difference in this world.

But Maude did think of making a difference. She looked out into the park across the street and saw kids smoking dope and drinking. She thought, *Maybe I could pray for them; maybe I could reach them; maybe I could talk with them about Jesus.* And she ended up leading kids to Christ and bringing them to her house for a Bible study. Later she opened a house of ministry on the other side of her duplex. Lives were touched because this old lady didn't think about herself and self-protection. She didn't let fear get hold of her. She was strong and courageous.

Or I could tell you the story of another one of my heroes, Delbert Keel. He's the man who led my father to Christ when they were both teenagers. Then both of them went off to war—my father with a gun in the Marine Corps and Delbert with a Bible as a chaplain. Delbert was a paratrooper who flew into frontline positions preaching the gospel and sharing Christ with the soldiers. They wrote books about the guy. He was a military hero in World War II. Why? Because he didn't let fear dominate him. He made a significant impact because he wasn't concerned with self-protection. Unless you can get past your self-protection you will never make much of a difference in this world.

Or I can tell you about Paul Bubna, my father-in-law, another one of my heroes. He was a pastor for many years and then at thirty-five he had a heart attack—it was so bad he had to have open-heart surgery. Things didn't look very promising. At forty-five he had another major heart attack. No doctor wanted to work on him, it was so bad. Finally he found somebody who would. He lived for twenty more years, and during that time he became the president of a seminary and a denomination. He could have easily protected himself and pulled back in fear; we wouldn't have blamed him. But he had such a significant impact on me and literally thousands of others. Why? Because he didn't follow fear. He was strong and courageous.

It would have been so easy for Paul Bubna, Delbert Keel and Maude Johnson to say, "I'm hurt; I'm damaged," and make excuses to protect themselves. Everyone can say they are damaged or hurt for some reason. We could all give reasons why we can't be used by the Lord. Moses would tell us to put those reasons aside and not to follow fear, but to follow the Lord. Be strong and courageous. That's how you're going to make a significant impact.

But most of us don't, because we buy our own excuses. Don't let fear and self-protection push you around. Instead, be strong and courageous. Get into ministry and start following the Lord instead of using excuses to stay out.

3. DON'T SEEK COMFORT

The third thing Moses would say is, "Don't seek comfort. Instead, seek to know the Lord and His power." I know that's true because he said basically that in Deuteronomy 34:

> Then Moses went up from the plains of Moab to Mount Nebo, to the top of Pisgah, which is opposite Jericho. And the LORD showed him all the land, Gilead as far as Dan, all Naphtali, the land of Ephraim and Manasseh, all the land of Judah as far as the western sea, the Negeb, and the Plain, that is, the Valley of Jericho the city of palm trees, as far as Zoar. And the LORD said to him, "This is the land of which I swore to Abraham, to Isaac, and to Jacob, 'I will give it to your offspring.' I have let you see it with your eyes, but you shall not go over there." So Moses the servant of the LORD died there in the land of Moab, according to the word of the LORD, and he buried him in the valley in the land of Moab opposite Beth-peor; but no one knows the place of his burial to this day. Moses was 120 years old when he died. His eye was undimmed, and his vigor unabated. And the people of Israel wept for Moses in the plains of Moab

thirty days. Then the days of weeping and mourning for Moses were ended.

And Joshua the son of Nun was full of the spirit of wisdom, for Moses had laid his hands on him. So the people of Israel obeyed him and did as the LORD had commanded Moses. And there has not arisen a prophet since in Israel like Moses, whom the LORD knew face to face, none like him for all the signs and the wonders that the LORD sent him to do in the land of Egypt, to Pharaoh and to all his servants and to all his land, and for all the mighty power and all the great deeds of terror that Moses did in the sight of all Israel. (Deut. 34:1–12)

Moses knew the Lord face to face. And if he was doing a seminar or writing a book, he would tell us not to seek comfort but to seek to know the Lord. Notice it says that the mighty power of God was not seen in anyone else like it was seen in Moses. What was the key to that mighty power? He knew the Lord. He made trip after trip after trip to the Tent of Meeting. And he would tell us that the key to the power of God in your life is to know the Lord. You need to know Him intimately.

Have you taken a trip to meet the Lord? How about this morning? Did you take a trip to the Bible, a trip to hear God and speak to Him? We don't have to go to a tent of meeting; we can just open the Scriptures. We can just pray. We have the Holy Spirit's presence in us if we are born again. We can come to God right now.

I wonder how many times Moses had to struggle with going to the Tent of Meeting, thinking, *I don't want to go there now; this isn't a convenient time.* But he decided not to seek his own comfort but instead take the trip to the Tent of Meeting and talk to God and hear God. He developed his relationship with God, so he knew the Lord intimately.

This is a key to Moses' life and the power of God in him. This is how he made such an impact. How badly do you want to know the Lord? Will you take a trip to meet Him every morning? Will you go to church? Will you join a small group? Reading the Scriptures, learning to pray and sharing your life with a body of believers are all ways in which you will come to know the Lord. It is the difference between whether you make an impact or not.

At a prayer luncheon I met an FBI agent, a committed Christian who had worked on many high-profile serial murder cases. I said to him, "You know, I've been wanting to talk with someone like you. I've got a question I've been wanting to ask for a long time. The Bible talks about a seared conscience—seared to such a point that you don't feel it anymore. Obviously, the people you've dealt with—serial murderers and rapists—don't feel anymore, right?"

He agreed, so I asked, "Can a person get to a point where he feels nothing at all anymore and becomes absolutely unredeemable? Have you ever seen someone who has done such evil things repent?"

He talked about some people who hadn't gone that far, in whom he had seen some genuine change, but in his opinion, true serial killers have reached a point of no return. I asked him how it happens that people get to that point. He said, "They have gotten so deep into their sin and are so deceived by the evil one that they are comfortable. They are absolutely in love with it; they find comfort in it, and they won't leave it. Is that a sick picture or what?"

The more we talked, the more it became clear to me that every one of us gets like that. Maybe we're not serial killers, but everybody has a capacity to do just what serial murderers do—get comfortable in their sin. Whether it's an addiction, a bad habit, the way you treat other people or lustful thoughts, you can get so comfortable in it that you won't leave it. My friend from the FBI concluded, "It's easy to point the finger at somebody like a serial killer, whose sin is so extreme, but all of us play the game."

Moses hit the nail on the head when he talked about not seeking comfort but seeking to know the Lord. And this FBI man drove the nail home when he said, "It's the only hope for your soul." It's not only true for a mass murderer or a serial rapist. It's true for you. Knowing the Lord is the only hope for your soul and your only hope to make any significant impact in life.

With this last chapter in Deuteronomy, we say good-bye to Moses. He climbs Mount Nebo and dies. We won't see him anymore, and we've learned so much from him. It reminds me of what I felt at my dad's funeral. This question came to my mind: *What will life be like without my dad in the world?* Immediately I thought of the answer: *My dad is still present here by what he passed on.* He knew Christ as his Savior, so he's with the Lord, but the only remnants of him left on this earth are what he passed on.

And that's going to be true of me and you. The only thing left of you is what you pass on, just as Stephen King said. What are you passing on? What are you giving away?

Or are you afraid of stepping out because of your injury, your problems, your sickness, your difficulty, your fear of other people? What's your excuse for not being in ministry? Moses would say, "Quit giving those excuses. Don't be afraid; step out. Be strong and courageous."

Moses, thank you; you've taught us so much. God, help us to listen, to move ahead and to learn from this wise old man.

ENDNOTES

Chapter 1

i.   Philip Yancey, *Reaching for the Invisible God: What Can We Expect to Find?* (Grand Rapids, MI: Zondervan, 2002), 61.

Chapter 2

ii.   Donald Grey Barnhouse, *Let Me Illustrate* (Old Tappan, NJ: Revell, 1967), 163-164.

Chapter 3

iii.   Gene Getz, *Moses: Moments of Glory . . . Feet of Clay* (Ventura, CA: Regal Books, 1976), 23.

iv.   Ibid., 24

v.   Flavius Josephus, *The Antiquities of the Jews*, Book 2, Chapter 9.

vi.   Maurice Wagner, *The Sensation of Being Somebody* (Grand Rapids, MI: Zondervan, 1976), 162.

vii.   Ibid.

viii. Ibid.

ix.   Bob Buford, *Halftime: Changing Your Game Plan from Success to Significance* (Grand Rapids, MI: Zondervan, 1995), 49-52.

x.   Ibid.

Chapter 8

xi.   Bob Buford, *Halftime: Changing Your Game Plan from Success to Significance* (Grand Rapids, Ml: Zondervan, 1995), 140.

Chapter 13

xii.   Maxie Dunnam, *The Communicator's Commentary: Exodus*
        (Nashville, TN: W Publishing Group, 1987), 166.

Chapter 14

xiii.   Charles W. Colson and Nancy Pearcey, *How Now Shall We Live?*
        (Carol Stream, IL: Tyndale, 1999), 311.

Chapter 15

xiv.   Aldous Huxley in *The Doors of Perception* as quoted by Dallas
        Willard in *The Divine Conspiracy: Rediscovering Our Hidden Life
        in God* (San Francisco: HarperSanFrancisco, 1998), 82–83.

xv.   Richard A. Swenson, M.D., *Margin: Restoring Emotional,
        Physical, Financial, and Time Reserves to Overloaded Lives*
        (Colorado Springs, CO: NavPress, 1995), 226.

xvi.   Ibid., 227.

Chapter 16

xvii.   Malcolm Muggeridge, "The Great Liberal Death Wish,"
        reprinted from *Imprimis*, Vol. 8, No. 5, May 1979, a publication of
        Hillsdale College. Used with permission.

Chapter 18

xviii.   Myron Rush, *Lord of the Marketplace* (Colorado Springs, CO:
        Chariot Victor Books, 1986), 152–153.

xix.   John C. Maxwell, *The 21 Irrefutable Laws of Leadership: Follow
        Them and People Will Follow You* (Nashville, TN: Thomas Nelson,
        1998), 181.

Chapter 19

xx.   As quoted in Charles W. Colson and Nancy Pearcey, *How Now
        Shall We Live?* (Carol Stream, IL: Tyndale, 1999), 253–255.

xxi.   Ibid.

xxii.   Ibid.

xxiii. Ibid.

xxiv. Dallas Willard, *The Divine Conspiracy: Rediscovering Our Hidden Life in God* (San Francisco: HarperSanFrancisco, 1998), 163.

Chapter 22

xxv. Stephen King, "What You Pass On," *Family Circle*, November 1, 2001, 156.

xxvi. Ibid.

This book was produced by CLC Publications. We hope it has been life-changing and has given you a fresh experience of God through the work of the Holy Spirit. CLC Publications is an outreach of CLC Ministries International, a global literature mission with work in over fifty countries. If you would like to know more about us, we invite you to contact us at:

CLC Ministries International
PO Box 1449
Fort Washington, PA 19034

E-mail: mail@clcusa.org
Website: www.clcpublications.com

DO YOU LOVE GOOD CHRISTIAN BOOKS?
Do you have a heart for worldwide missions?

You can receive a FREE subscription to
CLC's newsletter on global literature missions
Order by e-mail at:

clcworld@clcusa.org

or mail your request to:

PO Box 1449
Fort Washington, PA 19034

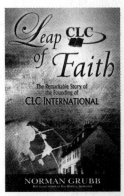

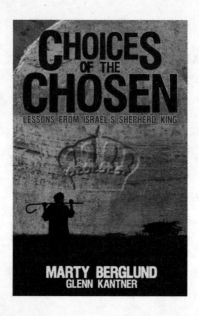

CHOICES OF THE CHOSEN

Marty Berglund and Glenn Kantner

"Just like David, we're the chosen. We're the anointed." The Biblical record of the life of David is filled with wonderful models for Christian living. *Choices of the Chosen* unearths these lessons, examining David's choices—the good, bad, and ugly—and applying them to the daily journey of today's follower of Christ

Trade Paper
Size 5¼ x 8, Pages 176
ISBN: 978-1-61958-056-5 - $13.99
ISBN (*e-book*): 978-1-61958-069-5 - $9.99